The
# ALIGNMENT QUEST™
# TOOLKIT
## for Activating Best Selves

by Laura Morgan Roberts, Ph.D.

Maximizing Best-Self Engagement,
One Strategic Choice at a Time.

*www.lauramorganroberts.com*

## Dedication

I dedicate this book
to the women in my lineage
who communicated through word and deed
the integrity of living in full commitment
to their best selves.
As business owners, educators, and community leaders,
Ethel, Norma, Joyce and Karen
demonstrated the power of bringing their best selves consistently
to every task life presented to them:
teaching, organizing, healing, exploring,
and most of all, in modeling the way
for my sisters, cousins, and me.

ဢ

## Acknowledgements

ဢ

This book contains the gems I have been collecting from nearly twenty years of research, teaching, consulting, and navigating my own career while advising others in their Alignment Quest™. I sincerely thank my collaborators, who have helped to build the intellectual scaffolding that undergirds the claims in this book. My colleagues at the University of Michigan's Center for Positive Organizational Scholarship have been especially important in helping me to discover and develop these guidelines for activating best selves. Thank you to Jane Dutton (who invited me to collaborate in this work as a graduate student in 2001), Gretchen Spreitzer, Emily Heaphy, Brianna Barker Caza, and Robert Quinn. Special thanks to Steven Shafer, Meghan Keedy, Karen Morgan, Judith Hawkins, and Christa Chambers Price, who reviewed early versions of my initial attempts to capture a set of interesting and applicable insights about reclaiming best selves. A very special thanks to my Alignment Quest™ course and retreat participants, who generously offered up their stories to activate their best selves. No writing project ever sees the light of day without the encouragement and flexible support of family members, and I am forever grateful to mine for helping me activate my best self, so that I could, in turn, help to activate the best in others. Team Roberts knows firsthand how many reams of paper, journals, lectures, workshops, and late nights have been poured into this project. Thank you for not letting me bury this work in the millions of to-do's that could have eternally distracted and diverted me from sharing this work!

ℬ

# Table of Contents

ℬ

മ

# Work-It-Out Exercises

മ

୫

# Introduction to The Alignment Quest™

୫

## ARE YOU LIVING IN ALIGNMENT WITH YOUR BEST SELF?

*Are you bringing your best self to your work?*
*Are you actively developing your strengths, weaknesses and principles*
*so that your best self will become even better?*
*Do you deliberately and consistently bring out the best in others?*

**Sadly, the vast majority of workers across the world will respond to these questions with a resounding "no." Instead of activating their best selves, most people bring their average, mediocre, or even worst selves to work.**

Reprinted with permission of National Arts Strategies and Jason Tseng.

&#8450; In the midst of pressures to accomplish more results with fewer resources, people are losing sight of their purpose and unique gifts. As a result, they fail to truly add value to their organizations and advance in their careers.

&#8450; Desirable jobs are increasingly difficult to obtain. For the sake of job security, many people are compromising their core beliefs, principles and health in order to maintain their employment or remain on a certain career track.

&#8450; Organizations are reconfiguring their roles, responsibilities, and status hierarchies at warp speed. In the wake of such rapid restructuring and downsizing, hyper-competitive workplace cultures are eroding social capital. Instead of fostering trusting developmental relationships and bringing out the best among colleagues, toxic working relationships bring out the worst.

&#8450; Technology allows for greater access to professional and personal networks. Yet, the opportunities for meaningful, authentic encounters between friends are few and far between.

&#8450; Fast-paced, round-the-clock flexible working arrangements blur the boundaries between work and non-work lives. "Quality time" is constantly interrupted by a barrage of emails, text messages, and news feeds.

&#8450; The affirming relationships with colleagues, friends and family that are necessary for strengthening and uplifting workers are left on the back-burner in favor of one more meeting, report, or presentation.

&#8450; People who temporarily modify their work roles (e.g., part-time, flex-time, or exit) in order to accommodate educational, career, or family interests face rocky transitions upon re-entry into this rapidly evolving world of work in nearly every sector. Instead, they engineer their careers to fit the new "gig economy."

In the wake of these challenges, people are finding it increasingly difficult – yet ever more important – to bring their best selves to work. The fact that the best self remains dormant and underutilized in most work settings is a hidden travesty of organizational life.

**Best-self alignment is the most promising pathway toward optimal living, but the everyday pressures of work and life often leave your best self by the wayside.**

While many working adults are merely trying to survive by keeping pace with unstable and demanding jobs, best-self alignment may seem far-fetched. And yet, it is absolutely necessary for **moving beyond surviving to thriving**. The Alignment Quest™ Toolkit will help you to understand why it is critically important to bring your best self to life.

Your best self is the most valuable resource that you will ever possess. Your vision of your best self is like a beacon of light that illuminates your path toward becoming the very best person that you can be. Remembering times when you were at your best can also serve as an anchor that keeps you from drifting too far away from the person that you are you meant to be.

## THE SECRET IS IN THE JOURNEY, NOT THE DESTINATION

We all have the potential for greatness. In times of scarcity and times of splendor, the human race remains passionate about self-actualization and living into our potential. But for many, that potential is never realized. This is why it has never been more important to demystify the process of bringing your best self to life.

**Most people do not have clear understanding of their best selves, fail to intentionally activate their best selves, allow their own insecurities to blind them to other people's best selves, and make life choices that lead them farther and farther away from their zone of best-self engagement.**

    &#8498; Do you wake up preoccupied with the multitude of things you hope to accomplish, but end the day feeling less productive and less fulfilled than you'd hoped?

    &#8498; Have you recently made a major decision or change in your life that you know will transform how you work and, consequently, how you live?

    &#8498; What if circumstances change, and shift you out of your best-self zone through restructuring, job loss, promotion, or technology changes that make your skills outdated? How will you respond?

The Alignment Quest™ is a process of continual learning and discovery. If the path to Alignment were well-trodden, we would probably be there already. There is always an element of mystery and adventure involved in The Alignment Quest™.

Before you turn another page, I must confess something to you. *I don't have all of the answers.* There, I said it. (You don't often hear a professor declare that she doesn't have all of the answers. But I would be misleading you if I told you that I did!) I can help you understand the common characteristics of best-self activation and alignment, but can't tell you who *you* are at *your* best in 150 pages of text. I can share with you some of the factors that help to bring best selves to life. But I can't tell you precisely which direction *your* career should take. I can't tell you what types of compromises *you* should make *right now* for the sake of *your* job security or future career goals. I can't tell you whether you should quit *your* job if you have one, or exactly what *you need to do to find a job tomorrow* if you are unemployed.

Starting your Alignment Quest™, and confronting many of the questions that it will raise, may surface the same feelings that I had in my recent closet-organizing project: excited, chaotic, overwhelmed and inspired! Let me explain. Have you ever noticed how when you are in the midst of getting things in order, sometimes things start to seem more chaotic than they were before you started "organizing" them? One hour into my closet reorganizing project, piles and piles of clothes, books, shoes, belts, scarves, and bags were strewn across my bedroom floor. I had pulled everything off of the shelves, and my attempts to create order were a bit overwhelming. This is what it may feel like when you grapple with your questions about living in alignment with your best self. Discovering your best self can feel like pulling out all of the items in your closet – leaving you surrounded by resources, but unsure about how to catalogue all of them in a way that is useful for you.

Fortunately, once I had initiated my closet reorganization project, a friend was there to help me to see it through by creating a new system for organizing, and then re-shelving the items one at a time. This Alignment Quest™ Toolkit is designed to be your companion, which will help you sort through the questions you are facing about how to bring your best self to life. The Alignment Quest™ experience, and the questions that it raises, will help you assess the various projects, relationships and dreams that are occupying your attention. Then, you will begin to design a new system for channeling your energy in the most fulfilling ways.

I may not have all the answers for you, but this book will help you to confront the most important questions in activating your best self. Based on my extensive consultations with thousands of accomplished and emerging global leaders, informed by intensive research on this topic, I have learned that the only way to discover the right answers is to pose the right questions about extraordinary living. The good news is that the answer isn't in the answer itself, but in finding the right Quest(ion)!

## CUSTOMIZING YOUR ALIGNMENT QUEST™

The Alignment Quest™ is a process of bringing coherence, purpose and joy to your life by learning how to create the most value in your daily living. The Alignment Quest™ involves both self-reflection and action. You will reflect upon the totality of your life, and consider whether key areas are in alignment so you are best equipped and energized to create value. You will then begin making a set of informed choices that can help shape who you are, what you do, why you do it, and the impact that you were designed to have on this earth.

Specifically, you will harness the power of your strengths and expand your impact. You will learn how to understand and embrace your strengths so you can better focus your energy. You will increase your capacity to accept your limitations so your attempts to be superhuman (or, all things to all people) don't lead you to make choices that are out of alignment with your best self. You can optimize your engagement and deepen your fulfillment at work. In short, you will begin to craft a life that is filled with extraordinary growth, vitality and value creation.

Extraordinary growth occurs when you are dedicated to a never-ending process of strengthening yourself and others to become your very best selves. Vitality emphasizes that your life is full of living – energized, meaningful, and uplifting. Value creation emphasizes that your life is sustained through mutual giving – making contributions that edify and strengthen social systems.

The Alignment Quest™ is a holistic perspective that focuses on YOU, your work and your world. You will be guided toward aligning your core purpose and passions with your work/career. Through these practices, you will begin to cultivate a system of support and resources that enhance this connection between who you are and what you do. You will deepen your self-awareness about the aspects of yourself and your life that are in sync with your career situation (current work) and career development (who you aspire to become). You will become equipped with the necessary techniques to hold yourself accountable for the choices you are making about the degree of alignment in your work and your life. And you will accept a certain degree of misalignment when there are tradeoffs to be made.

Your path toward best-self alignment is custom-made for you. It will not be like anyone else's. Yes, imitation might lead to short-term success. But when that season of lingering in others' shadows has ended, you will probably find yourself feeling even more fragmented. So get ready! The Alignment Quest™ will inspire you to courageously confront the fears and pressures that push you onto the brink of misalignment. Through this experience, you will begin to enthusiastically transform your hope-filled possibilities into your reality.

The step-by-step process in this book will help you to clarify and apply the core principles for activating best selves. You can decide the pace – and perhaps even the sequence – depending upon what works best for your career stage and life demands. You might spend more time on certain exercises in your first pass through this book, but you can return months or years later to revisit or delve into other exercises that are relevant in the future. There is no "one-size-fits-all" formula, nor is there a quick-fix or detour around the choices that you'll have to make.

But this book will aid you in making those choices in ways that maintain the integrity of your best self and that equip you to support others in doing the same.

## PRINCIPLES AND EXPECTATIONS

The Alignment Quest Toolkit is built upon ten important principles:

- **Freedom**. We have the freedom to pursue alignment with our best selves.

- **Learning**. We welcome opportunities to learn more about who we are and how we lead and live.

- **Resourcefulness**. It takes resourcefulness to maximize our opportunities for alignment with our best selves.

- **Interdependence**. Other people matter for increasing alignment – we can't do it alone.

- **Courage**. Alignment choices are not easy choices. We need courage to make these kinds of choices about activating our best selves and (re)crafting our lives.

- **Adaptability**. The Alignment Quest™ may involve moving from something more secure – a predictable, yet unfulfilling pain – to something less secure, but filled with promises of fulfillment in the long term.

- **Hope**. We act on the hope that today's Alignment Quest™ will give birth to tomorrow's promises. We undertake this Alignment Quest™ with a strong measure of faith that things are currently working together for good, anchored in our own experiences of transformation, success of fulfilled promises, realized goals, and grace.

- **Serendipity**. Our best self moments are a function of being in the right place, at the right time, while doing the right thing. This convergence of timing is often beyond our control. Many times our results have surpassed our input, and merit alone cannot explain why our risky choices resulted in tremendous gain.

- **Stewardship.** We strive to increase our own capability for contributing positively as citizens of a global society.

ဢ **Appreciative Inclusion.** We accept that various styles and approaches to leadership can be highly effective, when they are appropriate for the situation and the audience. However, no one style or approach will work with everyone, all of the time. Therefore, we recognize that each person brings a unique expertise for leading in a particular situation. The Alignment Quest™ requires openness and appreciation for the diversity among us.

## GETTING THE MOST OUT OF THIS ALIGNMENT QUEST™ TOOLKIT

Your output from The Alignment Quest™ will be a direct result of your input; you will get out what you put in to your own growth and development. The Alignment Quest™ will help you to begin a series of life-long transformations that require support, guidance, encouragement, fresh ideas and endurance. Those who have benefited most from this process have invested time and focused on deepening self-awareness through the readings, reflective exercises, and interactions with peers. We encourage you to undertake this Alignment Quest™ with professional or peer coaches.

The **Work-It-Out** exercises in this Alignment Quest™ Toolkit are your opportunity to begin reflecting upon the questions that are at the heart of the Alignment Quest™. So take them seriously. Pause, reflect, journal, commit and then share your experiences with those who can benefit from and support your Alignment Quest™. Take this opportunity to design new systems and experiment with new practices that will infuse your life with more clarity, synergy and purpose than ever before.

ജ

# Chapter 1:
# Raising the Bar

ജ

### *The race to be THE best.*

It dominates our attempts to succeed in a rapidly changing, hyper-competitive society. We are captivated by it everywhere we look – in sports, politics, popularity, beauty, dating, music, dance and other entertainment competitions. In the workplace we race to the top of organizations, industries, and the global economy. This race motivates us to push ourselves and our organizations to outpace the competition through innovation. The technology and tools we often take for granted, like cordless telephones, internet, wheeled suitcases, plastics, microwave ovens, seatbelts, cable television, home alarm systems, digital music, and athletic gear have helped to define industry leaders and to fuel our global economy.

And yet, the race to be THE best can produce dangerous side effects. Even winners can pay the price when the race to be the best goes too far. In a diverse world, focusing on beating the competition may actually take us out of our lane – and league – and into someone else's. We can start to lose our own sense of purpose and principles, by trying to chase someone else down the path to their dreams, when we would get much farther by charting our own path. Consider Olympic medalist Michael Phelps, who admitted that, even while he was the best in countless swimming events, he was far from *embodying his best self* during part of this victory season. Phelps struggled with depression, drugs and alcohol abuse, and was even arrested for driving under the influence in the years following his Olympic victories. Phelps' confession reminds us that being *the* best and being *your* best can be two very different experiences.

*The Alignment Quest™ requires that*
*We operate on a higher plane,*
*by Shifting the focus to our personal best —*
*Concentrating less on being <u>the</u> best*
*and more on becoming OUR best.*

Reprinted with permission of National Arts Strategies and Jason Tseng.

A parent gazes at a newborn child, a teacher greets a class for the first time, a CEO delivers a quarterly review to the entire company, a surgeon walks into the operating room, a supervisor walks around the shop floor, and a minister looks out upon a congregation. Each person wants the same things from the experience —to grow into their best selves and give their greatest gifts to the world, through their work, service, love —and to play an active role in helping others to do the same.

Instinctively, we want our children to be great, we want our companies to be great, we want our neighbors to be great, and we want our corner of the universe to be great. In these aspects of our lives, we believe that when people embody the fullest expressions of their best selves, our world will be a better place. But do we really know how to inspire and instigate the greatness that exists within ourselves and in others? Do we know how to help people to activate their best selves?

*At our best, We give strength.*
*We practice our virtues.*
*We leverage our identity-based expertise and relationships.*
*We experience positive self-regard &*
*We humbly pursue continued growth and development.*

## THE VAST MAJORITY OF PEOPLE STRUGGLE TO BE AT OUR BEST CONSISTENTLY.

- ℘ We are so used to thinking about our "typical" (or mediocre) self and our "worst" self, that we are still groping in the dark for a clearer picture of our best self.

- ℘ We lack adequate words to describe our best selves, and we have not learned how to deliberately activate our best selves effectively.

- ℘ Instead, we align with our typical selves, striving to meet externally-imposed performance metrics.

- ℘ We focus on demonstrating standard competencies rather than showcasing our distinctive strengths.

∽ We focus on abiding by social norms, even if it means undermining the ethical standards that reflect our best character.

Let's pause for a brief reality check. ***Are you bringing your best self to work every day?***

Gallup research shows the vast majority of people – between 70-80% of workers across the globe – are not bringing their best selves to work each day. When people are not doing what they do best on a regular basis at work, they begin to disengage. According to the Gallup Institute, workers who are disengaged dread going to work, have more negative than positive interactions with colleagues, treat customers poorly, tell friends what a miserable company they work for, achieve less on a daily basis, and have fewer positive and creative moments.

***Why are so few people bringing their best selves to work every day?*** For nearly two decades, I have sought answers to this question. Through research, coaching, consulting, and teaching, I have systematically examined the personal and situational factors that activate best selves and deepen workplace, community and family engagement. My research has uncovered a very interesting set of contradictions.

The first contradiction is between our assumptions about our own motivation versus other people's motivation to activate best selves. We have differing explanations for why *other* people aren't bringing their best selves to work versus why *we* aren't bringing our best selves to work.

The most common assumption about other people's underperformance is that *they aren't motivated*. I have led thousands of case discussions of leadership and talent management with managers and executives in search of the \*magic formula\* of potent incentives to motivate underperformers. Managers focus on accountability, oversight, penalties and prizes, expecting that these tactics alone will enhance performance. Yet, in many cases, their impact is underwhelming. When trust is lacking, these tactics actually have the opposite effect; instead of increasing motivation, they decrease it. Instead of inspiring best-self activation, they shut it down.

In fact, when asked to turn the lens on ourselves, and reflect on our own best-self activation (or lack thereof), we claim that we *are* motivated to bring our best selves to work. *Or, at least, we used to be motivated, when we felt valued and appreciated.*

What we currently lack are the opportunities to contribute to organizations from a position of strength. Every one of my coaching clients has indicated a heartfelt desire to bring his or her best self to work more often, and to make their best selves even better.

> *The struggle lies in*
> *aligning our strengths and values*
> *with the organization's needs and culture,*
> *and in receiving affirmation and development*
> *in our areas of strength.*

> *Most people desire to activate their best selves,*
> *but they keep getting "shut down."*

For example, I have worked with teachers who describe their "best self blockers" in this way:

> I have ideas about things we could do to help use differentiated learning techniques more successfully in the classroom. I've tried to encourage our principal to allow me to use grouping for reading or math in my classroom. But we decided at the district level that we don't do that. So, day-to-day, I see how I could develop and challenge a diverse group of children who have a wide range of abilities. But I don't have the opportunity to implement my ideas and suggestions anymore because of many of the outcomes that are being emphasized. They (administrators and Board members) are controlling the ways I have to use my time, energy and attention in the classroom. And their rigid policies don't leave room for my best self to activate.

Perhaps you can identify with both sides of this coin. There are likely times when you are wondering why somebody on your team is not motivated. At other times you may vent to your coworkers, managers or friends, *"Gosh, if I could only have the freedom, space or opportunity to try to do things differently – I feel like we could really make a huge impact!"*

So managers spend billions of dollars every month, hoping to find the right incentive that will encourage employees to bring their best selves to work, all the while placing their bets on management through fear and finances. And leaders push and punish their teams for losing ground to competitors, all the while losing sight of their most powerful *internal* lever for growth, development and performance: **best-self activation**.

The second contradiction is between our stated desires and our personal commitments to best-self activation. Many people don't even realize that they are living outside of their best-self zone. They assume that their current state of being is as good as it gets, and they don't expect much more of themselves or from others.

As people become further and further disconnected from their best selves, they adopt a mindset of stagnation, rejecting opportunities to grow and evolve, and instead, relying upon old mantras such as:

*We've always done it this way...*
*We've never done that before...*
*That will never work...you know how people are...*
*I don't see why we need to change things around here — they are good enough just as they are...*

Reprinted with permission of National Arts Strategies and Jason Tseng.

People who are trapped in stagnation define themselves in negative terms, they interact with others in a demeaning manner, and their insatiable desire to prove that they are "good enough" becomes a toxic element in their families and communities. Losing touch with our best selves is dangerous; we engage in destructive actions that undermine our best intentions and harm those around us. Activating our best selves requires courageous action – by countering our typical, fearful and comfort-centered approach toward living – and instead, striving to embody our full potential.

This book is designed to help you to do just that. The frameworks and exercises in this book will inspire and equip you to do the hard work of activating best selves: first, through discovering and developing your best self, and second, in bringing out the best in others.

Take your time with this book, allowing yourself the space to question your assumptions and past practices, and to consider developing new habits that will activate your best self and bring out the best in others. Striving to embody your full potential is a lifelong Alignment Quest™, which requires a personal commitment to continued growth, development and change – changing yourself and changing your circumstances. Knowledge of your best self will serve as a guidepost to aid your decision-making and fuel for your courageous journey of discovery.

Reprinted with permission of National Arts Strategies and Jason Tseng.

# WORK IT OUT!

## Exercise 1.1
## Best Self Activation Index
### ©Laura Morgan Roberts

**Instructions:** *How often are you at your best in your current job?*

Our best selves represent a fusion of the reality of our lived experiences - who we have been at our best - with the idealized sense of possibility for who we can be(come) when we fully embody our best selves. Focusing on our best selves fuels our hope, agency and empowerment. As we are reminded of all of the ways that we have embodied our strengths generatively in the past, we build confidence in our ability to make a positive difference in our own lives and the lives of others. Consider how frequently you actively engage your best self at work by answering these questions.

- How often do you <u>use</u> your talents in your current job?

- How often do you <u>use</u> your core competencies in your current job?

- How often do you <u>incorporate</u> your principles and values in your current job?

- How often do you <u>incorporate</u> your cultural background and experiences in your current job?

- How often do you <u>avoid</u> using your talents in your current job?

- How often do you <u>avoid</u> using your core competencies in your current job?

- How often do you intentionally <u>avoid</u> incorporating your principles, values or cultural background and experiences in your current job?

**How would you characterize your current level of best-self activation? (Check all that apply).**

\_\_\_\_\_ I feel disconnected and detached from my best self at work.
\_\_\_\_\_ I don't really think about my best self at work.
\_\_\_\_\_ I am actively working toward bringing my best self to work.
\_\_\_\_\_ I activate my best self regularly at work.

**Discussion Questions:**

ɛ) What did you learn about yourself from these questions?

ɛ) What self-knowledge was reinforced?

ɛ) How do you know when you are engaging your best self at work?

ɛ) What feedback do you receive when you are at your best?

ɛ) How often should people reasonably expect to bring their best selves to work?

ɛ) What is the role of leadership in increasing best-self engagement?

ɛ) What questions does this best self activation index raise about your Alignment Quest™?

ॐ

# Chapter 2:
## Discovering your Best Self

ॐ

Daniel is known as the go-to person on his job for IT systems, especially when problems arise and someone is needed to quickly identify and implement solutions. When Daniel is consulted for a trouble-shooting situation, one of two things could potentially happen. At his worst, Daniel communicates his expertise in a way that demeans everyone else who isn't able to solve the problem. Many of us have encountered people who become so consumed with excitement about what *they* know, that they are insensitive to their impatient style of communication. When asked for help, they say things like, "How could you *not* know how to fix this? Didn't they teach you this in training? You called me down here for *this*?" Lots of really smart people with a lot of expertise and experience are dismissive when others approach them for help. They are not creating a learning experience or environment, but, instead, are evaluative and judgmental in ways that make others defensive and resistant to feedback. When Daniel leaves other people feeling worse about themselves after interacting with them, even if he solves the problem, he destabilizes, devalues and disaffirms others' best selves.

But, Daniel has the capacity to enlighten and ignite best selves. A best-self moment occurs when Daniel uses his expertise to bring solutions, and does it in a way that elevates the experience that others have of themselves. After interacting with Daniel at his best, his teammates and clients feel like they are learning and becoming better. Daniel explains how he is solving the problem, involves others in the process, and therefore bolsters their confidence. After the interaction with Daniel's best self, coworkers and clients feel more empowered to solve similar problems in the future.

***At our best, we create value, not diminish value.***

We don't suck the life out of a situation with our grandiosity. When we are bringing our best selves, we edify, not terrify! At our best, our light illuminates the space around us, like a lantern helping others to locate their inner strength and talents as well.

Who are you at your best? What are your core strengths or areas of giftedness and principled leadership? How do you engage them in ways that promote vitality (for you) and value creation (for others)? I often begin my seminars with these questions, and I've heard thousands of people respond,

*"I'm not sure who my best self is!"*
*"What does it mean for me to be at my best, or bring my best?"*
*"Does it just mean for me to play to my strengths? Just do what I do well?"*
*"Is it the same thing as trying my best?"*
*"Is it the same thing as happiness, or loving my job?"*

Let's consider answers to these questions. My research and consulting have revealed the following: when we are in our best-self zone, we are making a meaningful contribution to something or someone beyond ourselves through our active engagement of strengths – our talents, core competencies, principles, identity-related experiences and insight.

We can live our lives in alignment with our best selves, our typical selves or our worst selves. Some people channel their talents and skills into activities that diminish rather than create value. Their actions are aligned with the values they cling to when they feel threatened, afraid and overpowered. They decide to ride others' coat tails or to take down other people in order to lift themselves up.

**Stagnation and suffering occur when we bring our lives into alignment with our mediocre, suboptimal, or worst selves.**

Periodically, one of my students or clients will propose that, instead of focusing on our best selves, we should spend our time identifying and remedying our worst selves. These leaders argue that, rather than focusing intensely on our best selves, we would be better served by identifying and reacting to our worst selves.

I have learned that this preferential focus on the worst self is fueled by our frustration with people (including ourselves) who are failing to embody their best selves. We see such great potential in ourselves and in others, and we are dismayed and disappointed by our collective failure to embody our best selves. We believe the best course of action to remedy human failings is to call attention to weaknesses, shortcomings and deficiencies. We attempt to establish intricate performance improvement plans and punitive measures to remind people of the damage caused by their darkest moments and to help them conquer their worst selves. We settle into our comfort zone – and focus on how "*everybody else* would be better served by working on *their* worst selves, so that they would stop infringing upon our best selves." Even when we reflect on our own performance, most of us spend far more time mulling over our mistakes than savoring our contributions and achievements.

So, we are really good at identifying our worst self, and pointing out the worst in others. But we are extraordinarily bad at trying to control and contain our worst selves. And despite all of these efforts, we are still left without a vision or a process for becoming our best selves. Avoidance and prevention do not yield the same extraordinary outcomes of growth, vitality and value-creation that are open to us when we embrace the full potential of our best selves.

Surprisingly, even in this self-aggrandizing, "look at me," praise craze, instant gratification culture that is permeating our society, *the best self is a mere illusion for some and a foggy haze or distant memory for others.*

My work with thousands of global executives continually reminds me of a shared human experience that transcends cultures: we are profoundly uncomfortable with holding up a mirror to our best selves. And we are even more uncomfortable with exposing our best selves to others' observations and characterizations. But this best-self avoidance becomes a self-defeating pattern of thought and action. Focusing on our worst selves will help us to break down our psyche, disrupt our practices, and deconstruct our situations, but it will leave us demoralized, lacking the inspiration or resources we need to construct the world in which our best selves can thrive and flourish.

*The TRUTH about best-self alignment is that it is equally, if not more important to focus on our best self than it is to focus on our worst self. Being blind to our strengths can be just as harmful as being blind to our weaknesses.*

First, when we don't focus on our strengths, we lack the intimate familiarity that we need to use them properly. Instead, we spend an inordinate amount of time trying to "fix" everything that is wrong with us, while we neglect those things that we are uniquely suited to do! Instead of leveraging our strengths to create value, we focus our attention on working on (or hiding, suppressing, downplaying) our weaknesses. Second, we miss opportunities to excel in the areas in which we might have the most potential, and inadvertently succumb to living a life in which we settle for being good, or perhaps even good enough... But we never quite reach the state of becoming extraordinary. Third, just using (misapplying) our strengths with no regard for our impact on others is dangerous.

Embracing the full potential of our own best selves is the only pathway to the growth, vitality and value-creation that we so desperately seek. We embrace this potential by transforming our mindset, practices and situations so that they call forth the best in each of us.

Our best selves are powerful containers of light and energy within us. The energizing properties of our best selves come from the fact that they are anchored in our strengths, rather than our weaknesses.

These strengths include our:

    &#8278; *Talents*, or naturally endowed features and abilities.

    &#8278; *Core competencies*, or personal skills and resources that enable us to add unique value to any situation.

    &#8278; *Principles*, or deeply held personal values about the appropriate way to accomplish our goals.

    &#8278; *Identity-based experiences and insight*, or the aspects of our personal backgrounds (e.g., culture, gender, education, profession, socio-economic class) that enable us to provide distinctive perspectives on organizational and societal issues.

Note that this broad definition of strengths includes skills and abilities, but also incorporates other attributes and experiences that reflect the essence of our uniqueness and distinctiveness. The skills and abilities that are encompassed in our best selves are exceptional; we are able to perform them consistently, distinctively, and creatively.

Think about the difference between Kerry, who sings along with the music while riding in her car, and Holly, a musical artist, who composes new arrangements while she sings and plays. Holly's best-self trajectory includes a creative dimension. This isn't to suggest that Kerry, or any of us who love karaoke are not musically gifted! The demonstration of our gifts *at their best* often include creative expression, as we offer something distinctive and valuable to others.

Our experiences and values are also important components of our best selves, because they enable to us to make valuable contributions to our workplace and our world. For example, when at his best, Carl exhibits the character strength of persistence in the face of failure. Syril's best-self moments reflect forgiveness in the face of disappointment. Kennedy, at her best, demonstrates the ability to reach beyond her own experiences to appreciate other's perspectives, and through this ability, she is able to understand other's needs, encourage other's dreams, and imagine new possibilities even in the face of obstacles. While diversity in strengths abounds, there is a unifying feature that characterizes everyone's best self:

*We are at our best when use our strengths in ways that make significant contributions, and, as a result, promote vitality and value creation.*

Being at our best energizes us and edifies others, putting into motion a virtuous cycle of giving that creates value within our social system. The star in the middle of this venn diagram points to the best-self sweet spot. This represents the moments in which we put our **strengths in action** to generative favorable outcomes for ourselves (**vitality**) and for others (**value creation**).

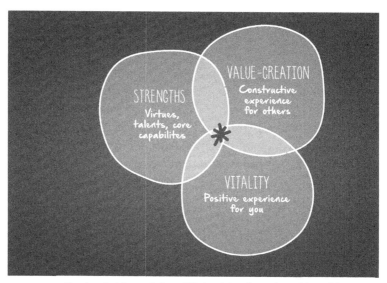

Reprinted with permission of National Arts Strategies and Jason Tseng.

Being at our best means drawing upon our sources of strength in ways that sustain us as we add unique value in the world. Best-self moments – those moments when we are at our best – create positive experiences for us. That is, the experience itself, or our memory of the experience, triggers any number of positive emotions, including: joy, gratitude, serenity, interest, hope, pride, amusement, inspiration, awe and love. Best-self moments aren't necessarily happy moments, however. Challenging, painful or difficult circumstances can bring out the best in us. Many people recall being at their best when they were battling serious illnesses, because they were focused on what really mattered to them, and they were determined not to give up hope for healing.

You can even activate your best self in difficult moments at home. Think about the parents who had to discipline their child for breaking curfew. The child probably didn't experience joy when both parents stood their ground and didn't allow him to attend the school dance as a consequence for breaking curfew. Yet, this may still qualify as a "parental best-self moment," if the disciplinary process helped to increase mutual understanding between the parent and child, and helped the child make better choices in the future. If the child felt demeaned and dejected, the parents' best selves didn't shine through as fully in this punitive experience. As long as learning and growth are taking place, best-self activation is effectively creating value for and through others.

Best-self moments can produce positive experiences for others, because people, families, organizations, and communities are strengthened in ways that are generative or life-giving. For example, Tina Turner is at her best when she creates a shared experience of vibrancy and enthusiasm throughout the audience. It isn't enough for her to be known as a great singer or dancer – the value-creation happens through the experience that they she is able to create for herself and others through the engagement of her strengths. Tina Turner was also at her best when she summoned the courage to leave an abusive relationship, trusting her inner power and strength to protect herself and her future.

Defining the best self often leads to judgment calls about integrity and impact. For example, people have asked, *"Was Adolf Hitler at his best as a leader during the Holocaust?"* Given that Hitler used his identity to bring about mass destruction, these actions do not characterize generative impact on society. Using strengths destructively rather than constructively do <u>not</u> constitute best-self moments. Refer to the following Work-It-Out exercises to discover more about your best self and how to activate it for vitality and value creation.

# WORK IT OUT!
## Exercise 2.1
## Best Self Appreciative Assessment
### ©Laura Morgan Roberts

**Instructions:** *What are your core strengths?*

To discover your best self, you need to conduct an appreciative assessment of yourself. *How are you (through your actions and perspectives) making a contribution that creates value?*

Most people have only a vague understanding of their strengths. (e.g., visionary – strategy or process implementation? Good memory of concepts, names, digits?) We often avoid talking and thinking about our strengths because we think it's an arrogant, egotistical, narcissistic excuse to rest on our laurels while we delude ourselves into a false sense of grandeur.

True, positive beliefs that are not grounded in reality can be dangerous. Yet, if we are really serious about studying our strengths, we will try to understand how we can leverage them effectively in the future based on what we have done in the past. By working from our core strengths, we increase our sense of efficacy and self-confidence. This gives us the energy and endurance we will need to make unique, valuable contributions to our workplace. If we are not using our strengths at work, it is very important to find some other outlet where we can put them into practice.

***Strengths are the qualities and characteristics you possess that enable you to consistently produce desired results.***

Consider the following sources of your strength.

- ✎ What are your talents, or naturally endowed features and abilities? Include an example of a time when you have used one of your talents to produce desired results. (Try to think of a work example, if possible).

- ✎ What are your core competencies, or personal skills and resources that enable you to add unique value? Include an example of a time when you have used one of your core competencies to produce desired results. (Try to think of a work example, if possible).

- ✎ What are your principles, or deeply held core values about the appropriate way to accomplish your goals? Include an example of a time when you have applied one of your principles to produce desired results. (Try to think of a work example, if possible).

- ✎ What aspects of your identity or personal background enable you to contribute a unique perspective to your organization? Include an example of a time when you have incorporated one of your identity-based perspectives to produce desired results. (Try to think of a work example, if possible).

# WORK IT OUT!

## Exercise 2.2
## Co-creating Value through Creative Contributions
### ©Laura Morgan Roberts

**Instructions:** *What are your creative contributions?*

You can deepen your best-self awareness by thinking about the different ways that you co-create value through your own creative contributions. Here is a list of several areas in which you might demonstrate strength through engaging your best self. Do any of them characterize what you do when you are at your best?

---

**The Arts: Increasing our appreciation of beauty in the world**

☐ Composing music

☐ Choreographing dances

☐ Writing plays, poems, or stories

☐ Creating artistic images, sculptures, paintings

☐ Creating culinary delights

☐ Designing fashion (apparel, interior decorating)

☐ Other examples:

**Organizing and Mobilizing: Making great things happen**

☐ Making plans through scheduling

☐ Making plans through process maps & how-to guides

☐ Making plans through financial savings, investing, and budgeting

☐ Creating inspiring visions, messages, and movement

☐ Other examples:

---

**Physical Activity: Encouraging health, fitness, and playfulness**

- ☐ Excelling in sports activities and events (individual & team)
- ☐ Engaging in disciplined exercise and/or nutrition routines
- ☐ Coaching and training with athletes (amateur and/or professional)
- ☐ Practicing holistic wellness activities (e.g., yoga, meditation)
- ☐ Embracing physical challenges for sport or fitness (e.g., mountain climbing)
- ☐ Building endurance in physical therapy following illness or injury
- ☐ Coordinating organized sports for fun (e.g., camping, bowling league, intramural basketball/swimming/soccer, tennis tournaments)
- ☐ Other examples:

**Products and Services:**
**Improving the health and well-being of society**

- ☐ Building structures and objects
- ☐ Inventing products
- ☐ Inventing technology
- ☐ Discovering medical cures and treatment plans
- ☐ Other examples:

**Relationships:**
**Bringing people together, and increasing healthy interdependence**

- ☐ Making connections through introducing people
- ☐ Making connections through emotional appeals (e.g., laughter)
- ☐ Building self-worth
- ☐ Creating family ties as a parent, child, sibling, or other relative
- ☐ Other examples:

# WORK IT OUT!
## Exercise 2.3
## Getting in the Zone
### ©Laura Morgan Roberts

**Instructions:** *What kinds of tasks do you find most engaging?*

When you show up to work, are you excited and enthusiastic about your work tasks? One way to tap into your best self is to identify the activities that send you into a flow–state, or zone of subconscious immersion. In the flow state, you become intense and focused on what you are doing in the present moment, you have the control and confidence to deal with intense challenges, and you experience the activity itself as intrinsically rewarding.

Think about the ideal range of activities that demand your effort on a daily basis: What types of work are both absorbing and energizing? Do you lose complete track of time when you are in the midst of those activities?

ഩ   Outside of your work, what activities can take you into the zone?

ഩ   Have you ever been "in the zone" at work? What activities have taken you there?

ഩ   What does it feel like when you are deeply engaged in your work. What are you typically doing? How do you know that you are engaged?

ഩ   What might help you to get in the zone more often at work?

**Discussion Questions:**

- ℘ Why is creativity important for best-self engagement?

- ℘ How often should people reasonably expect to make creative contributions through their work?

- ℘ What is the role of leadership in increasing best-self engagement through creative contributions?

- ℘ Which types of strengths (from the 4 categories listed above) receive the most attention in your workplace, family and/or community?

- ℘ Which types of strengths are most valued in work organizations?

- ℘ Which types of strengths can have the greatest impact on work organizations? Which can have the greatest impact on families? Which can have the greatest impact on communities?

**Key Insights:**

- ℘ What did you learn about yourself from these exercises? What self-knowledge was reinforced? What questions did they raise for your Alignment Quest™?

**Action Items:**

- ℘ What are the personal action implications of this chapter?

- ℘ What action items will you add to your developmental agenda?

- ℘ How will you use these exercises to help others?

ᔥ

# Chapter 3:
# Studying your Successes

ᔥ

Dawn's team had just come off a tough quarter. They had barely met their sales targets, after a last minute reorder from a long time customer pushed them above board. It was getting harder and harder to energize the team during their weekly sales meetings. So, Dawn decided to try a different approach. Instead of putting the shortfalls and disappointments in the spotlight, she decided to start calling out people's contributions – some of which helped to close deals, and others were the necessary "assists" to representatives who could then successfully attract or satisfy customers. After a while, the team began to pay closer attention to these types of contributions, noticing and acknowledging their teammates' positive impact, and even learning to provide their own examples and make stronger contributions based on colleagues' observations.

Most of us are uncomfortable when talking about our strengths and gifts, having been chided not to brag or boast. It can feel self-centered—even counter-cultural to focus on the positive. We also tend to seek and value deficit-oriented feedback because it helps us to feel that we are managing risks effectively. Our problems, deficits and shortcomings tend to have a stronger impact on our judgment, memory and emotions. Consider these social psychology findings:

- ജ It takes five good or constructive actions to make up for the damage done by one critical or destructive act.

- ജ The pleasure of gaining a certain amount of money is less than the pain of losing the same amount.

- ജ In character evaluations, it would take 25 acts of life-saving heroism to make up for one murder.

All of these statistics indicate that bad outweighs good.

Reprinted with permission of National Arts Strategies and Jason Tseng.

Even when we attempt to focus on possibilities, our well-intentioned mentors and friends might tell us not to get our hopes up, especially if the stakes are high and the competition is fierce.

*"Don't start dreaming about your new promotion just yet; there are a lot of strong candidates being considered. It took me four years before I was promoted to this level. You've only been in your current position for 14 months!"*

When we focus on problems, weaknesses and shortcomings, whatever looks promising on the surface is assumed to be too good to be true. In response, we counteract hopefulness with unhealthy doses of cynicism. Positive experiences and thoughts become like cotton candy in our mouth. They just sort of fizzle away.

For example, think of a performance evaluation conversation that you had with a supervisor. Even if 99 of 100 comments were positive, that one biting comment or harsh criticism became seared in your memory. I still recall a few of the comments I have received on my teaching evaluations – especially the hurtful ones, such as one that I received when I started teaching at Harvard Business School at age 27: "*I really think a leadership professor should have more REAL-LIFE experience.*" Ugh!

You might hold onto negative comments for decades. But the positive comments? Ask yourself two weeks later – what were some of the GOOD things that your students said about you? What were some of the positive things that your manager or supervisor told you in your conversation? You'll probably muster a vague recollection, "*Oh, well, my manager told me I was doing a pretty good job*, BUT..." Positive comments are hard to articulate. But the negative comments and feedback? We remember them word for word.

We also tend to minimize our own contributions and actions. Instead of embracing our best self moments, we casually state that "it was no big deal," "anyone could have done it," or "I just got lucky." We don't want to take undue credit. We don't believe our current actions measure up against our memory of who we used to be, or our idealized images of who we think we *should* be. We won't pat ourselves on the back because we are waiting for someone else's acknowledgement. When we minimize our contributions, we write ourselves out of our narratives of success. These misguided attempts toward humility lead us to denigrate our best selves. As author and mystic C.S. Lewis wrote, "True humility is not thinking less of yourself; it is thinking of yourself less."

*The best-self zone requires us to think about how we can be a contribution to others through the principled engagement of our strengths. We are intentional in our focus on values and capabilities, and we dedicate them toward the greater good when we are at our best.*

Discovering our best selves requires putting on the hat of a scientist and collecting evidence of positive impact. Like an archeologist, we must go on a search for our best-self moments – looking for traces of our demonstrated strengths and cultural clues about our meaningful contributions. Like social psychologists, we can examine our interactions with others, testing our hypotheses about the types of situations, people and mindset that help to activate our best selves.

Imagine how strong we would become if we were to study our successes as much as we ponder our failures? It's unlikely that we will be our best selves *all* of the time. But we can certainly aspire to be at our best more often, and to make our best selves even better. Through systematic observation of our best-selves, we can achieve this goal.

We can begin activating our best selves by taking one success story at a time. **Think about one time when you used your strengths to generate desired results and positively impact the world around you.**

Don't let this memory flash by too quickly. **Don't oversimplify the success.** Write it down; spend time recounting the details in your journal. Give a play-by-play account what happened, where it occurred, how you felt, and what kind of feedback you received about your actions and interactions.

These memories may come from your distant past, or they may have taken place as recently as today. These moments may have occurred during family interactions, schoolyard encounters, professional tasks, community service/civic engagement, church involvement, or athletic competitions. Don't worry about whether they are grand enough, momentous enough, or impressive enough to qualify as a "triumphant story." **Begin where you are, when you use the best of what you have been granted to positively impact the world, no matter how small the effort may seem.** This storytelling exercise will help you refocus your energy on becoming your best self. Over time, you will compile more and more stories that will change the tone of your narrative from the deficient to the proficient, and from stagnant to flourishing.

## THE REFLECTED BEST SELF EXERCISE™

I love to read the life stories of Superheroes. Some of the most exciting, significant, dramatic and memorable moments precede their life-saving acts of heroism. Do you remember when Peter Parker first encountered Spiderman? When Clark Kent first discovered Superman? When Diana the princess first put on her golden wristbands and Wonder Woman belt to deflect darts and bullets? When Forest Gump ran so fast that his leg braces flew off? When these Superheroes first discovered their unique strengths, they embraced them, marveled at them, and used them to benefit their world? But none of these superheroes, like none of us, would have discovered those strengths if they hadn't been stretched.

We face critical moments that jolt us into deeper awareness of the power of our strengths – such as facing an illness, taking on a new assignment at work, or speaking out for our beliefs. In these moments, we are called to rise above our typical state of being and perform or contribute in ways that leave a lasting impact.

We discover the significance we play in someone else's life by doing what seems to come naturally to us. Strengthened by the realization that we matter, at our best we are like superheroes in our shared capacity to touch the world in profound ways.

To develop a deeper understanding of your best self, it is important to solicit feedback from others about how they experience you at your best. **The Reflected Best Self Exercise™** (RBSE) is an innovative leadership and career development feedback tool for helping people to discover and leverage their strengths. With my colleagues at the Center for Positive Organizations, I have shared the RBSE with thousands of emerging and established leaders in premier executive education programs, corporate talent management initiatives, required and elective Masters-level and undergraduate degree programs, professional development seminars, adolescent internship programs, and family and friendship circles. The *RBSE* uses a multi-step process to help people discover and activate their best selves. This process involves reflecting upon moments in a person's life when he or she was at his or her best, examining these best-self episodes closely for cross-cutting themes and variations, and composing a best-self portrait (written or multimedia) that captures the essence of the qualities and behaviors a person exhibits when at his or her best.

The most valuable aspect of the RBSE is gathering "contribution stories" from colleagues, clients, friends and family members, which allows understanding of an individual's best self as reflected by those who know him or her best. These contribution stories about best-self episodes can be task- or relationship-based, past or present, personal or professional. This important step in the exercise should be pursued carefully, using the detailed, self-guided instructions that have been developed for the RBSE, and working with a facilitator, coach or teacher to apply key insights.

The instructions for completing the RBSE are available on the Center for Positive Organizations website (www.positiveorgs.bus.umich.edu).

Some people are hesitant to seek *RBSE* feedback, because they are concerned that other people may perceive them as arrogant. Yet, the exercise proves to be a valuable learning experience for all ages. The majority of my clients and students receive feedback from 60%-70% of the requested providers, and many of the providers express their apprcciation for the opportunity to share how someone has made an important contribution. Less than 5% of the feedback providers express concerns about the exclusively positive focus of the exercise, or submit feedback that describes people's weaknesses instead of their contributions.

Activating our best selves is a life-long journey. We may have potential strengths that we have not yet recognized or utilized. As people receive positive feedback about their contributions, they heighten their awareness and deepen their understanding of their best selves on an ongoing basis. Best-self insights often emerge in spontaneous and unexpected ways. Someone might compliment you during a meeting or organize a retirement party for you. You might be called upon to take the lead in a situation when you weren't expecting to do so, but your efforts will yield successful results. By leading effectively, you develop new skills and earn credibility that might offer additional opportunities for new projects. If you are studying your successes, these experiences will help you to notice and recognize the contributions you are making. Knowing who you are at your best can help you to take advantage of these moments—or even create them—no matter how they present themselves.

**IT'S NOT *ALL* ABOUT YOU…**
**BUT IT DOES BEGIN WITH YOU!**

Many self-help books will persuade you to focus only on your own feelings and ideas, as if you must exist in a private bubble of positive thinking in order to experience happiness. Your thoughts and feelings do shape your identity, which includes your best self, typical self and worst self. But, your identity doesn't just exist in your own head or heart. It is influenced by the interactions and feedback that you receive from other people over the course of your lifetime.

We learn about our strengths (and our weaknesses) through evaluating the results of our efforts; and while our personal opinions matter a great deal, the feedback that we get from our environment helps us to validate the accuracy of our own opinions. We are at our best when the activation of our strengths generates positive experiences for us (which only we can assess) *AND* constructive experiences for others. The experience of the other person can only be understood through respecting their point of view, acknowledging that it may differ from our own, and receiving and honoring their feedback.

In short, your best-self zone is NOT all about you as a stand-alone actor. Nor does it exist in your head as a source of personal pride and self esteem, with no connection to your everyday actions. Your best self is made real through the exercise of virtue and strength for a greater good. Your understanding of your best self is informed by social experiences that shape your sense of self as a valuable contributor to your family, community, organization and other social systems. The more you learn about your best self, the better you will understand your impact on others and your surroundings, and what others love and/or value about you. Redefining your best self will require you to develop a more sophisticated understanding of the social world around you.

If you think this process is all about you, you may miss key signals about whether certain conditions are calling forth or inhibiting your best self. You will probably find that it is easier to be your best self in some situations than in others. There are some people who bring out the best in you, and others who may activate your worst self! Some tasks inspire you to fully engage your strengths, while you merely tolerate other tasks long enough to fulfill the stated requirements. This is important to notice. You will not always be able to choose your surroundings, tasks, coworkers, or even family members.

It is unrealistic to expect that you would be at your best at all times, especially when facing these kinds of obstacles. However, your mindset will make the difference when your worst self is leading you to live down to the lowest common denominators of greed, deceit, and pride rather than live up to your best self-potential. The goal is to harness the power of your strengths to expand your impact, optimize your engagement and deepen your fulfillment at work. Understand and embrace your strengths so you can better focus your energy. Accept your limitations, so your attempts to be superhuman (all things to all people) don't lead you to make choices that are out of alignment with your best self!

Life doesn't revolve around only you, so there is no room for self-absorption and arrogance in your best self. But the process of activating your best self does begin with you, and your willingness to redefine your best self, realign your actions to reflect your best self, and redesign your life to nurture your best self. As you raise your awareness about the social conditions that shape your ability to be at your best, you will humbly accept your personal responsibility to bring your best self to life.

# WORK IT OUT!
## Exercise 3.1
## Best Self Reflections
### ©Laura Morgan Roberts

**Instructions:** *How do you activate your best self?*

When we are at our best, we activate our strengths in a principled manner; we use our strengths in accordance with our values and principles to generate positive experiences that are gratifying for us and edifying for others. Think about all of the different strengths you possess (e.g., talents, core competencies, strengths of character), and how you have used them responsibly to produce desired results.

- ℘ Can you a recall a situation in which you *displayed virtuous qualities?*

- ℘ Can you a recall a situation in which you *controlled your impulses and kept your ego in check?*

- ℘ Can you a recall a situation in which you *adapted effectively to new circumstances?*

- ℘ Can you a recall a situation in which you *stayed true to yourself, by acting in accordance with your values or principles?*

- ℘ Can you a recall a situation in which you *made a unique or distinctive contribution to your team, family, or community?*

- ℘ Can you a recall a situation in which you *helped others to recognize and affirm one another's strengths?*

- ℘ Can you a recall a situation in which you *bridged differences among people, by helping people to build new connections or fostering greater understanding of differing points of view?*

    🙵  Can you a recall a situation in which you *persevered in the face of a challenge?*

    🙵  Can you a recall a situation in which you *received feedback that indicated that your best self was affirmed, understood and appreciated?*

    🙵  Can you a recall a situation in which your *worst self was forgiven through your exercise of virtues?*

    🙵  Can you a recall a situation in which you *experienced yourself living up to your full potential?*

**Describe an image, story, song, dance, or film that relates to one (or more) of your best-self moments.** How does it relate to your best self?

## Discussion Questions:

    🙵  How often do you give and receive strengths-based feedback? Is this a conscious choice?

    🙵  What did you learn about yourself from these exercises? What self-knowledge was reinforced? What questions did they raise about your Alignment Quest™?

    🙵  What feedback do you receive when you are at your best?

    🙵  What are the personal action implications of these exercises? How can you learn from past experiences of activating your best self?

    🙵  What needs to happen for you to activate your best self more consistently? What action items will you add to your developmental agenda?

    🙵  How will you use these exercises to help others?

∽

# Chapter 4:
# Reclaiming your Best Self

∽

Nicholas was among those fortunate enough to find his right out of college. He started his first post-college job under ideal circumstances. He was selected for his top choice job at a well-known company. He turned down 3 other appealing offers from reputable companies to take this position. Optimistic, and somewhat naïve, he carried his hopes, dreams and plans with him into this new position. Enthusiastically, Nicholas tried to bring his best self – and to put his best foot forward – during the interview and initial entry period.

Nicholas was a top candidate on the job market based on his high profile internships throughout college. By the time he started at the company, he had already developed a few valuable relationships in the industry. Nicholas hit the ground running and experienced early success in his career. With a few "wins" on his track record, he was soon dubbed a rising star in the company. However, he didn't let the success go to his head. He remained open-minded, humble and curious. As a consequence, his best self was recognized and affirmed; he was regarded as an up-and-coming mover-and shaker, on his way to greatness, and his success and genuine concern for others inspired them to do the same.

Like Nicholas, many people begin their working careers filled with hope and optimism, excited by the opportunity to earn their *own* money! Working - under fair and just conditions - is a sign of independence, and a step towards a desired future. We imagine ourselves progressing in our careers, moving from the lower ranks of salary, autonomy, and influence to gain more status, benefits and impact as we learn and grow.

Unfortunately, the pitfalls, competing commitments and distractions of our professional and personal lives lead many people away from this vision of becoming our best selves and living our best lives. Day by day, encounter by encounter, and decision by decision, we lose touch with our best selves.

Imagine what happened to Nicholas' best self when he became overwhelmed with the demands of multiple pressing deadlines, the lack of collaboration between his teammates, limited resources for staffing his boss's pet project, and preparation for his upcoming wedding. His boss began hinting that he was concerned that Nicholas wouldn't be able to meet the pending deadline for a key client. Then, when Nicholas submitted a project proposal with a few errors in the work process flowchart, his boss berated him in front of the entire team. By the time of Nicholas' wedding, his former C-suite supporters began to wonder aloud whether he had what it took to advance to the next level in the company.

Nicholas, who had been so excited about engaging at work, began to feel devalued, and he lost sight of his best self. As the days passed, he forgot about his unique strengths, and could only focus on trying to cover up or compensate for his weaknesses. After a few years in this climate, Nicholas became cynical, frustrated and exhausted.

Nicholas' reaction is not unique. Most people's best selves falter when they feel ignored, denied and rejected by other people. To cope with this rejection, they pour our energy into other people's agendas, and compromise their ability to give fully to what matters most.

Like Nicholas, what we think we are doing for success may, in fact, undermine our survival in the "Fake it 'til you make it!" and "Winner takes all!" career management games. We convince ourselves that we will have the luxury of focusing on our best selves once we are established enough, secure enough, rich enough, popular enough, and confident enough. Relying on other people's advice, we believe that our compromises will pay off over time. One hopes that as we grow older, we also mature, becoming wiser about who we are and what we need. But too often, through our commitments and promises, we trade off on our own best selves for short-term gains. We bargain away the identities that matter most to us and keep us most connected to our best selves. So we lose sight of the most valuable and meaningful parts of our identities. We lose touch with our best selves.

Even people who, on the surface, seem to have everything under control may feel disconnected from their best selves. Instead of realizing their strengths, people are walking around with memories of their "Epic Fail" moments figuratively tattooed in 3D across their hearts. For example, we carry beneath the surface the crushing rejections of former friends and relatives, who criticized the way we walked, talked, dressed, and lived. These types of words and encounters become seared in our memories, casting a shadow of doubt over the very best of who we are and who we can become.

How do we typically respond to identity threats that undermine our best selves?

*Rather than tapping into our own sources of strength to build up a more positive, stable identity, we embark on a never-ending path of proving that we are "good enough;" attempting to prove that we deserve our job, our title, our accolades, our friends, and more chances to prove ourselves!*

Sadly, when the proving game fails to bring us the success and fulfillment we desire, many of us begin to deceive ourselves and other people. We pretend that we are strong in areas in which we are weak, and we remain weak in areas in which we could actually grow stronger. We are tempted to ignore our personal best, while seeking to advance through more titles, responsibilities, recognition, and compensation.

Many people begin to move out of their own areas of giftedness in pursuit of what appears to be a promotion into leadership – a chance to be "in charge" – even though they might have greater influence and impact by demonstrating excellence and engagement where they are strongest. And, once they assume the leadership role, these same people often fail to develop a new set of strengths that are required to coordinate the efforts of their team and chart a compelling vision for growth and impact. Instead, many new leaders struggle because they naively overplay their strengths as individual contributors – trying to do everything for their team, and pretending to have all of the answers – instead of learning to delegate and get things done through others. Over time, these leaders' strengths become weaknesses that inhibit their own effectiveness and cripple the development of their subordinates and partners.

**Fear also leads us away from our best selves.** When we are afraid, we live beneath our potential. Our misconceptions about growth and development lead us to concentrate our efforts on beating out the competition rather than becoming our best selves through meaningful, lasting contributions. Quite frankly, we ignore our best selves because we choose the safe route toward growth and development: learn the rules of the game, develop the skills to play the game, knock down or side step the obstacles, and know that the winner-takes-all.

We are inundated with social guidelines, rules and expectations. We busy ourselves with making the grade, passing the bar, and measuring up – all of which orient us toward developing in accordance with external standards. We seek to prove that we are good enough; good enough to belong to our community of choice, to keep our jobs, to remain in solid academic standing, to earn a bonus for the next year, or, at the very least, to avoid being eliminated from the competition altogether. The risk of losing our status, our relationships, and our resources leads us to vigilantly scan our environment for people and circumstances that harm our sense of security.

We fear that if we dare to dream about what we might accomplish through exercising our strengths, we will take our eyes off the problems that are lurking around us, and, in our ignorant bliss, they will consume us. We passionately demean what's wrong in the world, in other people, and in ourselves rather than inquiring into what's right. We pay the costs of living beneath our potential every day, as our souls yearn for the rhythmic dance between the world's longing and each person's giftedness. And yet, we choose to remain blind to our best self, and the possibilities that it brings for true transformation. We are playing it safe in damage-control mode, thinking and talking about problems, instead of embracing possibilities.

*This is the real travesty of neglecting our own best self;*
*It isn't just a personal problem,*
*It's an organizational problem and a social problem.*

When we are feeling depleted and insecure, and our identities are unstable, we aren't able to focus on helping others to become their better selves. In our insecure state, we are too threatened by others' talents to affirm and support their extraordinary potential. When we are feeling threatened, all of a sudden the game changes. No longer are we in the space of trying to become our own best selves, and celebrating our own best selves. Instead, the game has changed into proving who is *the* best, which is a zero sum game (e.g., only one person can be the smartest in the room, so we focus on building a reputation as the most knowledgeable, even if this involves demeaning others' intelligence.) When playing the zero sum game of winner-takes-all, we act on the assumption that in order for us to become better, someone else has to become worse. We project our insecurities onto others, and destabilize their trajectory toward becoming their best selves as well.

We lose touch with our best self during different seasons in our lives. So, to reclaim our best selves, we must "retrace our steps" through self-reflection, which helps us determine when and how we lost touch with our best selves.

Dana, a managing director MD on Wall Street, discovered after her 40 year career trek, that she'd "dropped" her best self characteristics along the path to success. While she was clutching the ladder to success so tightly on her climb to the top, her best self slipped out of her hands. At the time, she was too afraid of falling backwards to reach out and grab her best-self features. Dana's reclamation process involved retracing her steps back to the place when she last felt intensely connected to her strengths and contributions. Like Dana, we may need to sort through the "lost and found" repository of developmental experiences, in an effort to help us to reclaim our best selves.

Christoff's best self was hijacked by his own ambition – his ego jumped into the driver's seat of his career and family, and took over; he become a helpless passenger on the fast track to fame. As he looked back over his life, his choices had been dictated by other people's desires and values, as they defined what he should and could become. Like Christoff, we may need to reclaim our best selves from the oppressive fear of rejection. We may need to let go of proving we are "good enough" to break the barriers of becoming our best selves.

Shayla gave her best self away in an unhealthy relationship with a romantic partner; Therese sacrificed her best self to her employer's needs and Rolf traded his best self for his addiction. All three people were continually denied the affirmation and appreciation they needed most. But, for the sake of comfort and security, they stayed in these unhealthy relationships. Shayla, Therese and Rolf's reclamation process took them back to the dumpster, to dig through the drudgery of cruel words and dehumanizing actions, in search of the gems that they were created to become. Likewise, we will need to shake off shame, as we draw strength and hope from the vision of who we are becoming and recognition of how far we have come.

During the reclamation process, we have to reflect on our best selves. We have to reexamine the moments when we acted from a position of strength. We have to re-narrate ourselves, as we start to tell different stories about our place in the world; stories about who we are and our sense of significance, while broadening the possibility for where we can go. Then, we recommit to growing and developing in that process, by cultivating necessary resources.

The good news is many of these resources come from within. As we understand more about our sources of strength, we experience positive emotions. These positive emotions help us to increase our sense of agency, optimism and hope. Ultimately, this process positions us to see more possibilities, to build stronger relationships, to co-create new opportunities to access physical and financial capital and, as a result, we can experience best-self engagement.

Initiating the reclamation process may be like getting reacquainted with an old friend. As we spend time focusing on our best self, we experience the nostalgic reminders of other times we've been fully engaged through glimpses of our past. Through the reclamation process, we become more curious to find out what has happened to our best selves over the years, and we'll eagerly anticipate where our best selves might lead us in the days and years to come. As we become more attuned to our best selves, we are liberated from the need to prove our worth through status comparisons and rankings. We begin to evaluate our best selves based on our meaningful contributions to other people's growth and development. When we reclaim our best selves, we inspire and empower others to do the same.

The best-self pathways toward becoming extraordinary challenge the belief that success is achieved on the battle ground between winners and losers. Instead, the best-self paradigm opens new possibilities for virtuous cycles of growth and contribution. The more we understand and engage our best selves, the better equipped we are to help others understand and engage their best selves.

*This journey is bigger than us;*
*It is about more than our identities, our hopes, and our dreams.*
*As we actively engage our best-selves,*
*we co-create the conditions for others to do the same.*

When we reencounter our best selves, we shake off the shameful existence of feeling deeply disconnected from our hopes and dreams. We no longer have to live in regret, fearing that our better days were behind us. The result – the very act of self-acceptance, understanding and ambitious drive for growth serves as an invitation to other people around us.

Reclaiming our best selves liberates us from the constraints of others' standards and expectations. When we are insecure and doubtful, we are too busy finding the flaw to help create the flow. As we become more confident in our own strengths, we are less threatened by others' strengths. Greatness flows through us, as we surrender our need to be superhuman and openly acknowledge our personal limitations.

The bottom line is that we can't do it alone. Why does our interdependence matter so much for best-self actualization? Why do we need to pay attention to how we treat each other, and the impact that it has on our best selves? We can't overpower other people's best selves and then expect to reach our full potential. We can drive performance or compliance through force, but we can't force authentic best self engagement. The best self is not invoked by mandate, dictate, fear, or frenzy. Only inspiration can nurture its emergence. When the best self is activated, we enter into a sacred space of reverence for both our distinctiveness and our common humanity. The most powerful result of discovering and embracing our best selves is the transformative power it has on others around us.

Reprinted with permission of National Arts Strategies and Jason Tseng.

# WORK IT OUT!
## Best Self Blockers
## Exercise 4.1
### ©Laura Morgan Roberts

**Instructions:** *What are your best-self blockers?*

Think about a recent work experience in which you **struggled** to function at your very best. Write the story of what happened, including how the episode got started, what kept it going, and how it came to an end.

- ℘ Why was it so difficult to bring your best-self to light in this situation?

- ℘ What does this tell you about the conditions and mindset that activate your best self?

- ℘ How did your best-self struggles impact other people in this situation?

- ℘ If you could rewind the clock, would you change anything about how you responded to these challenges to your best self?

# WORK IT OUT!
## Best Self Trajectories
### Exercise 4.2
#### ©Laura Morgan Roberts

**Instructions:** *What is your current best-self trajectory?*

*REFLECT UPON YOUR PAST.* Over the course of your life, have you been motivated and equipped to <u>strategically deploy</u> your best self?

ဢ   Think back to your prior jobs. Did they bring out the best in you? Were your strengths valued by the organization? Knowing what you know now about your best self and the situations that bring out your best, is there anything you would have done differently?

ဢ   Think about the relationships in your life. Who has played a key role in helping you to grow? Who has helped to advocate for you when other people may have overlooked the potential in your best self?

*MAP YOUR CURRENT TRAJECTORY.* Imagine that you continue your current approach toward best-self engagement for the next 10-20 years of career.

ဢ   What will become of your best self if you follow this trajectory? What will be the trademark of your career along the current trajectory?

ဢ   To what extent is your best self in alignment with the standards, expectations, and needs of your institution, profession, and industry?

ဢ   To what extent is your best self in alignment with the career path that you have been pursuing to this point? Does a deeper understanding of your best self change your desired career path?

ဢ How would you work and live differently, if you were building a platform or "franchise" based on your best contributions?

**Discussion Questions:**

ဢ What are your typical responses to best-self struggles?

ဢ What are some of your most helpful responses to best-self struggles?

ဢ What is the role of leadership in minimizing and/or addressing best-self struggles?

ဢ How can you seek out more best-self enablers?

ဢ How can you limit your exposure to your best-self blockers?

ဢ How can you create the conditions that bring out the best in you and in others?

ဢ What did you learn about yourself from these exercises? What self-knowledge was reinforced?

ဢ What are the personal action implications of these exercises?

ဢ How will you use these exercises to help others?

ဢ What questions do these exercises raise about your Alignment Quest™?

educator

# Chapter 5:
## Maximizing your Contributions

educator

educator

Despite organizational innovations, there seems to be a widening disconnect between people's desire to contribute maximally from positions of strength, and the opportunity to do so. Here's the scenario. On one hand, most people think they are working really, really, really hard every day – constantly on the verge of burnout. And yet, far too few people feel they are making valuable and significant contributions. Most people feel they have more to offer than they have the freedom to contribute, because their best selves aren't activated.

It seems that we are facing a paradox of work engagement. A paradox refers to a state in which two things that seemingly cannot coexist, such as polar opposites, occur simultaneously.

## PARADOX OF 21ˢᵗ CENTURY WORK ENGAGMENT

**People are**
**Overextended**
**and**
**Underutilized**
**at the same time!**

It's ridiculously absurd that these two things could be happening at the same time, and yet, they reflect the reality of organizational life.

Think about the person who is so preoccupied with "busy work," fire- fighting, and loose ends that there simply isn't time to cultivate her strengths and feed her purpose. For example, many teachers spend so much time dealing with disciplinary issues in their classrooms, they lack the time and energy to introduce innovative and impactful curricular changes.

Technology contributes to this feeling of busyness; we read the same emails ten times, browse articles through social media outlets, and respond to a few text messages and updates around the clock, 24 hours/day, 7 days/week, 52 weeks/year.

Other times, we fail to be selective in how we invest our time and energy. We overcommit, by taking on too many projects and committees, and then we under-deliver on the results because we are spread too thin. As the saying goes, we become a "Jack of all trades but Master of none." Like hamsters on a wheel, we haven't made considerable progress. At the end of the day, we are even more overextended and underutilized. Being busy, even when you're doing very important work, is not the same as making meaningful contributions. Meaningful contributions connect your strengths and your daily tasks with your own sense of purpose.

Reprinted with permission of National Arts Strategies and Jason Tseng.

Organizations must shoulder some of the responsibility for this paradoxical existence as well. Although the image of "busy worker bees" comes to mind, this is actually a romantic ideal; it assumes that each bee is performing a specialized set of tasks so the system can flourish. Unfortunately, our modern organizations are filled with workers who are underemployed, misguided, and on overload.

Consider the following scenarios:

- The relentless attempt to "do more with less" often results in overloading workers, like doubling up job assignments after downsizing or reorganizations. People who are already stretched too thin are pushed toward the verge of incompetence when managers assume they can handle the responsibilities of their own job <u>plus</u> those of their former coworker(s) and/or managers. Streamlined organizations are creating more generalists, which may come at the expense of best-self engagement.

- Gifted sales people, customer service representatives, care providers and technicians may be inundated with paperwork. When IT systems aren't integrated, and cross-functional exchanges aren't occurring smoothly, people are burning candles at both ends to manage redundancies in organizational systems.

- Many university professors are teaching an overload of courses in order to meet financial obligations and/or colleagues' preferences, which doesn't allow time for mentoring, reflecting, sharing best practices of curricular design, or piloting new courses. Teaching and research are also pit against one another in the battle for scarce resources, and most faculty have little time to share their research findings with the people who can benefit most from them.

හ Medical doctors and nurses carry heavy patient loads, with financial incentives to treat patients as quickly as possible. Opportunities to explore the patient's personal context and holistic health history, provide culturally competent care, and consult with other care providers are scant.

හ Junior level consultants are assigned to support partners on cases; working long hours and traveling long distances, but are only involved in the implementation stage of the project. Despite their potential insight about clients' needs, they are considered too "green" to bring viable strategic planning suggestions.

හ The chief of police of a local district has 14 officers on duty during each shift, and they are responsible for covering 50 square miles of dense residential and commercial territory. In one week, there were ten aggravated assaults in this area, and each one required 2-5 officers to respond to the situation. Clearly, these local officials are overextended by responding to distress calls, at a time when they are needed for strategic planning for public safety and community peace building initiatives.

In these contexts, where learning is essential, organizations try to do more with less and jeopardize best-self engagement as a result. Instead of recognizing the Paradox, managers and workers become consumed with their deficiencies and underperformance, which creates a downward spiral of depleted morale and escalating defensiveness. Exasperated, they give up on best-self engagement, and focus on making it through the crisis of each day. Survival becomes the name of the game.

*When you are immersed in the Paradox,*
*it's nearly impossible to imagine thriving.*
*And yet, that's exactly what we must do.*

In order to bring our best selves to work, and experience the meaning and significance we seek in life, we have to do the exact opposite of what you might expect. Even though we are overextended and underutilized, *we must find ways to stretch farther, but in the right direction.* We fuel the desire to grow, becoming better and helping other people to do the same.

This requires adopting an agentic mindset toward value-creation. In other words, we have to recognize opportunities to exercise choice in how we spend our time and expend our effort.

*In essence, we must become more astute about when, where and why*
*we take on projects, roles, and assignments, using a best-self lens*
*to invest in the greatest potential for value-creation.*

When we are able to activate our best selves, we are also able to maximize the value of our contributions at work, in our families and in our communities.

How can we use our best self-activation lens to aid our decision-making about future opportunities? How does understanding our best-self characteristics help us determine when to say yes and when to say no? First, we must learn to selectively embrace mediocrity, by accepting "good enough" in some areas to pursue greatness in others.

# BALANCING "GOOD ENOUGH" WITH GREATNESS

Will "good enough" ever lead you to greatness? Can you become your best self, even if you are comfortable with being good enough?

The answer to both questions is: YES!

It's true that short cuts and easy outs won't help you activate your best self. The just-enough-to-get-by mentality may have been enough to earn passing grades in school, but the real world is full of so many tests, we can't possibly slide by all of them.

Yet, some people are stuck in mediocrity in every aspect of life: they study *just enough* to get by, they call or show up *just enough* to make sure they aren't forgotten, they work *just enough* to avoid disciplinary action, and they contribute *just enough* to be seen as competent.

> *An across-the-board attitude of mediocrity*
> *will not get you anywhere worth going in life.*
> *But neither will an ego-driven pursuit*
> *to reach perfection in everything.*

The only way to become your best self is to choose your domains of excellence wisely. Then, you'll have to let some things go in the other domains of life. You can't succeed in being the ultimate corporate citizen who shows up early, leaves late and plans all of the social events for your team, *and* also become the ultimate P.T.A. member who attends every field trip and volunteers in your child's classroom one afternoon each week.

Just as you choose your domains of excellence, you must also choose your domains of mediocrity. That is, you must decide in which areas of life "good enough" is, in fact, good enough. For example, you may choose to be a mediocre navigator: to know *just enough* to get around the city and use your navigator if you get lost. Perhaps you have chosen to let your piano-playing skills fall by the wayside. Maybe your years of studying French will linger only in dusty schoolbooks and faint memories of vocabulary words. You may enjoy running or swimming daily, even though you may never reach Olympic status! That doesn't mean these activities aren't worth pursuing. You can choose to participate for the love of it!

When it comes to activating our best selves, some things have to give. Sure, we can invest more time in honing our skills in many different areas. But sometimes we have to choose, given the limitations of time, energy and other resources. In these situations, we can utilize the **Contribution Calculation Framework** to help guide our decisions.

Ask yourself, how much value will this endeavor create, relative to my other investments of time and energy? For instance, you might create even more value by spending an extra hour with your pre-school daughter or teenage mentee to help them develop language, music or critical thinking skills than you would create by joining your coworkers at happy hour. Or, perhaps you will create the most value by honing your skills to pursue a new career path, instead of working tirelessly on tasks that you don't find stimulating or meaningful.

Reprinted with permission of National Arts Strategies and Jason Tseng.

## LET <u>MAXIMAL CONTRIBUTIONS</u> GAUGE YOUR INVESTMENT DECISIONS

When you take a full inventory of your strengths, you must decide which activities are worth investing your time, talents and treasures, and which tasks should be delegated to others or relegated to your peaceful acceptance of "good enough."

*Striving to be extraordinary in <u>everything</u> only increases your anxiety about never being extraordinary in anything.*

*The path to the best-self alignment lies in being content with "good enough" in some areas and in some moments, while working strategically and wholeheartedly to raise the bar in others.*

79

So when the next opportunity comes your way, you can use this Contribution Calculation Framework to help you determine your potential for value creation, by assessing degrees of alignment between the demands of the role, task or assignment, and what you are able to contribute from a position of strength. Most important, realize you have a choice in how much of yourself you will invest in any given opportunity! Then, ask yourself these questions outlined below, to help you to choose wisely.

It is easiest to understand the Contribution Calculation Framework when you apply it to your current situation. So, I'd like you to pause and consider: a) an opportunity that you might pursue, b) an assignment or role that you might accept, or c) a recent commitment that you've made.

*Think about a new career opportunity that you are considering pursuing or have recently accepted. This opportunity might involve changing, adding or developing new a project, assignment, task, role, relationship, or even employer.*

The guiding question that we will explore is:

*At present, am I motivated and equipped to fully activate my best self in this opportunity, assignment, role or commitment?*

Answering this question requires you to consider what drives you – what is your core purpose and what are your strongest priorities? How do they align with this opportunity, assignment, role or commitment? Then, you'll need to consider how to invest your resources of time, energy and core capabilities to maximize your contributions and create the most value.

Reprinted with permission of National Arts Strategies and Jason Tseng.

Now, let's walk through the four pillars of commitment, capability, capacity and then contribution to help you decide how much of your time and energy to invest in this opportunity. We will start with the first pillar, which is Commitment. The questions below will help you assess the depth of your commitment to activating your best self in this opportunity.

## ~ PILLAR 1. COMMITMENT ~

*Consider* your DESIRED IMPACT.

- ❧ What do you hope to gain through making this change? (Your desired impact could include: learning, growth, career advancement, or benefit to others.)

- ❧ What are the results you wish to create?

- ❧ Is this an opportunity for you to dedicate your effort toward a desired end? Will it help you to accomplish your broader goals for leadership impact?

*Assess* your level of CARING for this opportunity.

- ❧ How deep is your commitment to making a significant contribution in this area?

- ❧ How deeply do you care about this opportunity?

- ❧ Which of your core values are aligned with this opportunity?

- ❧ How passionate are you about this opportunity?

- ❧ To what extent are you dedicated to pursuing excellence and producing extraordinary results in this area?

- ❧ What are you willing to sacrifice in order to bring your best self to this opportunity?

These questions are important because the process of activating your best self to maximize your contributions will demand an open-hearted, open-minded embrace of your optimal state of being. At your best, you are exceeding your common, ordinary, comfortable state of being. You are stretching beyond your typical set of activities that keep you in your zone of safety. You are breaking the default thought patterns of deficiency and lack, and instead cultivating a mindset that embraces your potential and the abundant resources that you are capable of accessing and even generating. Reaching this optimal state of being requires consistent dedication toward manifesting the best of what is possible, *even when* your internal and external dialogue continually remind you of obstacles, hardship, and disappointment.

You must have a compelling reason for showing up as your best self. In Nietzche's words, *"One who has a why to live can bear with almost any how."* Humans seek meaning and significance in our work; we want to believe that our efforts are not in vain, and that our toil and triumphs matter to something or someone outside of ourselves. We work harder when we believe that what we are doing matters to someone that we have encountered. People who interact with the beneficiaries of their work efforts are more persistent and productive, even in mundane and challenging tasks, than those who are disconnected from the beneficiaries of their work effort.

Engaging in work that is personally important enhances vitality, as evidenced by reduced stress, depression, turnover, absenteeism, dissatisfaction and cynicism, as well as increases in commitment, effort, engagement, empowerment, happiness, satisfaction and a sense of fulfillment. While there is no such thing as a "perfect job," clarity of purpose helps to identify new pathways for best-self activation and value creation.

### *Why do you work?*

Work is an all-inclusive term that refers to a wide range of activities, paid and unpaid, that involve expending effort toward a specified end. We all WORK at something. In fact, we are all workers in many spheres of activity. Even if you aren't receiving a paycheck for certain activities, your efforts still count as work. Thus, when you think about bringing your best self to work, I encourage you to redefine yourself in the context of this wide scope of activities. If you are retired, how do you channel your best effort in your community work? If you are a domestic administrator (my preferred term for the outdated concept of "housewife") are you bringing your very best to your efforts to care for your family and manage the affairs of your household?

**Circle all of the words below that describe your "work" activities, paid and unpaid.**

Building relationships
Managing your household affairs
Caring for loved ones (seniors and youth)
Fighting for social justice
Serving those in need
Maintaining physical health or athletic prowess
Learning
Self-improvement
Disseminating information
Entertaining yourself and others
Developing new products
Selling to interested clients
Growing a business
Increasing social awareness
Practicing your faith

People who have a compelling reason for showing up to work are more motivated – and more capable – of experiencing vitality and value at work. You may put forth effort in a variety of activities, but whenever we label something as "work," we begin to focus on what the activity demands of us. Take a minute to think about what you are *gaining* from working. Do your work activities provide?

- Stability
- Security
- Opportunity to build meaningful relationships
- Stepping stone for future opportunities
- Chance to learn more about your work and about yourself
- Other benefits?

Pause and reflect upon *why* you work. You might also ask yourself the following questions, and write down the answers. Review them daily to deepen your commitment at work.

- Why did I show up to work today?
- Is there a purpose (a task, a cause, a relationship, a community) that I consider to be worthy of my best effort?
- Do I have other compelling reasons for working, even if my best self isn't being invigorated through my current activities?
- If I don't have a compelling reason for channeling the best of myself into my work, do I have an alternate set of activities that draw out my best self?

*If you are out of alignment with your best self, because your sense of purpose is unclear or waning, how long can you sustain this degree of misalignment?*

## ~ PILLAR 2. CAPABILITY ~

The second pillar focuses on Capability. This pillar captures how much this opportunity will tap into your core strengths. The questions below will help you assess how capable you are for activating your best self in this opportunity.

*Analyze* your CAPABILITY for bringing your best self to this new opportunity.

- In what ways are you equipped to make a contribution?

- How are your strengths aligned with this opportunity?

- How have your previous experiences prepared you to succeed on this task?

- How have your prior successes validated your ability to grow into this role as needed?

- Do your key stakeholders believe that you have the **credibility** needed to consistently deliver strong results in this role?

- Are your strengths valued in this **context**?

It is important to understand your capability because of its impact on your work engagement. The Gallup Institute surveyed over 10 million people worldwide on studies of employee engagement, and found that one of the strongest indicators of engagement is whether or not respondents agreed with the statement, "At work, I have the chance to do what I do best every day."

But only 20% of the people who completed this questionnaire agreed or strongly agreed with that statement! This study indicates that people who put their strengths to work on a daily basis contribute to their organizations in profound ways, as evidenced by higher engagement (6x as likely to be engaged), higher life satisfaction (3x as likely to report excellent quality of life), lower turnover, higher satisfaction for the employees, and higher satisfaction for customers who interact with members in those units who are highly engaged and bring their best selves to work every day. Organizations whose employees "do what they do best everyday" have 1.5x higher productivity than typical organizations.

Another Gallup poll showed that not a single person who reported *not* having a chance to do what they do best everyday was emotionally engaged on the job. People who are less engaged dread going to work, have more negative than positive interactions with colleagues, treat customers poorly, tell friends what a miserable company they work for, achieve less on a daily basis and have fewer positive and creative moments.

## ~ PILLAR 3. CAPACITY ~

Pillar 3 focuses on Capacity. This pillar captures how much time and energy you can devote to this opportunity, given the other life obligations you must fulfill and the amount of resources you have to support your work. The questions below will help you assess how much capacity you have to activate your best self in this opportunity.

*Analyze* your capacity to contribute your best effort at this time by conducting an inventory of your bandwidth and resources. Can you devote the necessary time, energy, and attention to this new opportunity?

ဆာ Are you available to devote your time and energy toward applying your capabilities with excellence?

ဆာ Do you have the bandwidth to commit to the process of learning and developing new skills that may be needed in this role, assignment or opportunity?

ဆာ Can you rely upon others to assist you in generating the necessary resources to maximize your contributions? Do you have the buy-in needed for maximal impact?

This holistic assessment is important for grounding your aspirations in the reality of your current commitments. No matter how much we care, or how capable we may be, we cannot squeeze our best-self moments into our spare time. Maximizing our contributions demands our time and effort, especially when we take on "stretch" assignments that require learning and growth (building capability) or that tap into our core values and passion.


## ~ COMBINED EFFECT: YOUR CONTRIBUTION ~

The fourth pillar, Contribution, represents the combined effect of your Commitment, Capability and Capacity. Based upon your analyses of the first three pillars, what is the likelihood that this opportunity will bring out the best in you? What is the likelihood that it will position you to bring out the best in someone else?

Answer the following questions to Calculate your Potential Contribution from undertaking the new role, assignment or opportunity you are considering in this exercise.

- ဆ Will you make a valuable, positive difference through your dedicated effort?

- ဆ Will your engagement increase your level of personal vitality?

- ဆ How much value will you create by engaging in this work, versus affording someone else the opportunity to do so?

- ဆ How much value will you create by investing time and energy into this role versus investing my time and energy elsewhere?

Many leaders have found this exercise to be powerful for organizing their daily and long-term commitments. One leader was able to gain clarity on the importance of making time for a weekly dinner with his aging father. Another leader was able to decide between two very attractive job offers: one was an internal promotion, and the other was at a company she'd always wanted to join. She ultimately decided to remain with her current company, accepted the internal promotion, and immediately began to seek opportunities to apply her strengths in building relationships to her new role with facilitating organizational change initiatives. Because time is, indeed, our most precious resource, it is important to make the most of opportunities that increase our vitality and help us to create value by contributing to others' quality of life. I encourage you to utilize the Contribution Calculation Framework to help you align your investments with your best self potential!

# WORK IT OUT!
## Life Hacks for Best Self Engagement
### Exercise 5.1
#### ©Laura Morgan Roberts

**Instructions:** Here are some ways that you may need to restructure your life to increase your best self engagement. Try designing a 21-day experiment that involves changing your everyday habits or practices, and testing your assumptions about best self engagement, using the prompts below.

### Prioritize to increase your capacity.

so Into which activities will you channel your creative ingenuity and commitment for the next 6 months? Over the next 3 years?

so How do your current life and professional circumstances influence your best self activation in the short term and longer term?

so Are energy-depleting activities consuming a lot of your time and resources? Can you remove them entirely, or minimize the time you spend on them?

**Recalibrate: Dial back your energy investment in tasks that are misaligned with your best self, and turn up your energy investment in tasks that are more aligned with your best self.**

so Plan your weekly schedule for best self activation. Schedule your personal commitments in protected blocks of time (e.g., choose 3 nights when you will try to sleep 6+ hours, because this is critical for your best self activation). Set a goal to carve out more time in your week to work on the ideas or personal projects that are at the cornerstone of your vision of the ideal/career/personal trajectory.

- Plan your daily schedule for best self activation (consider micro-level, everyday practices that can shift your mindset, emotion or reality, such as dinner without devices, workouts, email cut-off times, regular social routines, volunteer service) in order to do more of what energizes you in high-impact ways.

- During your highest energy periods of the day, or week, work on the tasks that are energy-depleting. You will be able to complete them with greater confidence and efficiency when you energy is high. You need more energy to pour into them, because they don't typically generate many energy returns. The goal is to "get it done" according to the needs of the end-user. These may be the tasks in which "good enough" will suffice.

- During your low energy times of the day, work on tasks that are aligned with your best self. They will energize you.

- Add daily rituals to foster the inspiration and mental/spiritual clarity needed to optimize efficiency and impact. Make an intentional choice about how to build in leisure, especially the activities that can give you more energy to activate your best self during other points in the day.

**Discussion Questions:**

- How does your Contribution Calculation influence the way you think about leadership development? Talent management? Career planning? Energy management? Team-building?

- What is the role of leadership in building capability within organizations?

- What is the role of leadership in strengthening courageous commitment within organizations?

- What is the role of leadership in increasing capacity for best-self engagement within organizations?

ຂ

# Chapter 6:
# The Best is Yet to Come

ຂ

Take a step back. Think "big picture" about where you are in your path of growth and development.

**Are you striving toward optimal existence?**
**Are you pursuing your full potential?**
**Are you a better human being now than you were several years, months or even days ago?**

In the words of Mahatma Gandhi, we must ***"Be the change [we] wish to see in the world."***

This means it is time to stop waiting for things around us to change. We must stop waiting for the world to invite us, beg us, or push us into becoming our best selves. It is time to stop waiting for other people to tell us that we are good enough. It is time to stop expending our best energy trying to convince other people that we are worthy of their company or esteem. It is time to let go of the pressure to obsess over other's impressions of us, and to stop playing "the blame game" when life isn't going our way.

**Let's take the initiative on raising the bar for ourselves,** by taking the lead in living into our own positive expectations. It is time to let go of our damage-control mentality, and have a love affair with our best selves. It is time to find out what we love most about ourselves, and grow from that intimate understanding. We don't have to be perfect; we only need be genuinely committed to humble service and continual growth.

**We fully reclaim our best selves when the story of our lives – as told in the present – ends with the belief that "The Best is Yet to Come."**

In order words, to become our best selves, we must we see ourselves as growing, maturing, adapting, evolving, or progressing in a positive direction. Whether we know it or not, we each carry in our heads and hearts a *metanarrative* about our journey toward best-self actualization. A metanarrative is a broad or overarching story about a collection of experiences that have taken place over time. Our metanarratives of best-self actualization feature our storylines about how we have grown closer to our best selves in some situations and phases in life, and farther away from our best selves at other times. Our metanarratives are important because they frame best-self actualization as an ongoing process of emergence that unfolds day-by-day and step-by-step. Our metanarratives establish a point of reference for where we are in life, compared to where we think we should be, could be, or have been. Our metanarratives also capture our future expectations; describing our anticipated growth and development --- such as, where our lives may lead and who we may become in the future.

In our most transformative metanarratives, we project a future version of ourselves that is *becoming* more like our best self, and less like our worst self over time. The concept of *becoming* is especially important here --- we must embrace the never-ending journey toward best-self actualization. Perfection isn't required or desired, but a commitment to growth is essential for bringing our best selves to life, while also bringing out the best in others.

Take, for example, Gabby Douglass, the first U.S. Olympic gymnast to win all-around (individual) gold and team gold during the same Olympic year. When Gabby was only 11 years old, she believed in her own potential as a gymnast, despite the fact that she didn't have elite gymnast training. She told her mother that if she could work with the coach who had trained other Olympians, she was sure that she could win, too. And she was right!

Ballerina Misty Copeland also persevered in her extraordinary giftedness, despite the fact that her family didn't have financial resources to support her training, and her curves and brown skin were criticized as a hindrance to her dancing ability and stage presence. Yet, Misty Copeland believed in her potential, even when many of the so-called experts did not. She became the first African American performer to be appointed as a principal dancer for the American Ballet Theater in 2015, at the age of 32, after dancing through severe injuries over 15 years at ABT. Misty Copeland's meta-narrative of best-self actualization is captured in her quote, **"You can start late, look different, be uncertain, and still succeed."** In recognition, Mattel released an official Misty Copeland Firebird Barbie in 2016, as part of its SHERO's collection which celebrates women who "have broken boundaries, challenged gender norms and proven girls can be anything they want to be," according to the company's press statement.

Becoming also involves making decisions to change course when necessary, in order pursue our growth potential. Oprah Winfrey recounted a point in her early career when, as a reporter in Baltimore, she had compromised the health of her body (and hair!) in an attempt to take on an inauthentic persona as a "mainstream" newscaster. Despite her accommodations, she was told that she was "too emotional" for the job. Then, in the early years of hosting her talk show, Oprah faced a moment of truth when featuring members of a domestic terrorist group, who were using their appearance on her show to promulgate messages of hate. She decided, at that moment, that she would never allow her message to be compromised by the never-ending competition for ratings. More recently, when she launched her OWN cable network, she had to confront her core purpose and align it with her platform once again, after taking the reigns to turn around poor ratings in the first year.

Although professors are often looked to for their expertise, we also have to undergo the process of reclaiming our best selves continually. During the recruitment process, new faculty are widely heralded as rising stars who are expected to thrive as scholars and teachers. Yet, many early career professors struggle to publish their research while adjusting to faculty life. They are often blindsided by poor teaching ratings and rejections from the editors of their desired publication outlets. In academia's world of subjective evaluations, being labeled as "struggling" constitutes a fall from grace. Yet, when a junior faculty member, Alisa, found herself on this path, she changed her internal narrative by reminding herself that she was audacious and brave. She began setting boundaries, so she would have the space to focus on her research. Alisa fully committed to co-creating the conditions that would allow her brilliant best self to thrive and flourish.

Quite the opposite of Alisa, many people surrender to defeat when faced with these kinds of struggles. Instead of pursuing future best self-engagement, they take on self-defeating rhetoric. Here's one version from a popular movie, *"I could've been a contender!"* You may have heard a version that sounded like this from a relative, neighbor or former classmate: *"When I graduated from high school I was a star athlete… But then I had to take a job working at the post office so that I could play the bills. So I'll never be my best self. I believe my best days are behind me."* Sadly, some people recast their entire life in terms of their current travails, and conclude that their glory days have come and gone. They may find it difficult and painful to remember times in their lives when they were at their best, because they feel like those days are behind them. In fact, as a professor, I've even heard college students lament hopelessly that their best days are behind them (as in, high school!), and that life will be downhill from here.

Seth was a 20 year old college student who confessed, in tears, that he could not participate in a class discussion about his best self because it was too painful for him to remember how far he had drifted away from it. Tara also burst into tears when I asked her to engage in a similar discussion; at the age of 50, she announced to her colleagues in a workshop that she did not have a best self. While Tara and Seth may have turned away from their best selves, others in their lives were eager to "shine light on what was right" within each of them. They left our sessions feeling more whole and more hopeful than they had felt before. They were on a path of becoming – not returning to the former self, but growing into their best selves.

How can we establish a stronger sense of self - a more positive identity - that helps us to build connections with others and transform our life and world? How do we stay connected with the reality of our shortcomings, without completely ignoring, hiding, or burying our gifts and talents?

It's a choice. Plain and simple. Just like everything else in life. We can allow our words, thoughts, and deeds to shovel pile upon pile of dirt upon our best selves, burying them deeply in fear, anxiety, and ego defensive routines. Or we can keep digging… Keep searching for remnants of best selves, reassembling our positive identities one encounter or choice or story at a time. Remember, the most powerful narrative isn't about becoming better than *anyone else* – it's about becoming better than our former self, and closer to our potential.

In this sustainable narrative, we say to ourselves,

"The Best is Yet to Come!

I am part of a never-ending process of becoming,
characterized by peaks and valleys,
courageous choices and inspired resilience
to continue pursuing best-self actualization.

I'm learning and growing from my past mistakes.
I get better, not bitter.

I innovate to make creative contributions
in different stages of life.

Becoming my best self is a humble pursuit of ongoing
growth and service.

In order to enter my best self zone,
I must fully embrace the fact that
I DO matter,
I AM uniquely gifted,
and I am a work in progress,
with an UNLIMITED CAPACITY
for making my best self even better every day."

Best-self activation also requires shifting our orientation from self-preservation to generation and contribution. In our ego-defensive state, we attempt to lay claim to the larger share of virtues and accomplishments, as if there is a scarcity of goodness in the universe, and we must guard our share and status to prevent someone else from stealing from us. When we are still in denial of our own best selves, someone else's expression of best self activation can even become threatening; through social comparison, we seek to tear them down in order to fuel our false sense of pride. When we become preoccupied with proving our own self-worth (to ourselves or to others), we become less open to feedback that can facilitate the level of growth required in best-self activation.

As we focus on actualizing our own potential to be our best, we relieve ourselves of the burden of competition to be THE BEST. That is, our identity isn't dependent on our comparisons of being better or worse than other people. We recognize our own unlimited capacity for growth, and we become more enthusiastic about granting greatness in others.

## ACTION PLANNING

We can adjust and realign our thoughts and action continually, so they reinforce our best selves. Action-planning deepens the impact of self-reflection by advancing our developmental agendas for generating extraordinary outcomes in organizational contexts. Knowledge of our best selves is grounded in the reality of our prior contributions, not in idealized, unattainable images of who we hope to become.

Within an action plan, best-self activation is framed with moderate expectations; we may not always be in the best-self zone, but our action plans will give us clear ideas about what we need to do to get there more often, and to have greater impact during our moments of best-self activation.

You may want to pursue multiple paths, but an action plan for best-self engagement will help you to pick the domain of excellence in which you will soar. Action planning can also help you to guard yourself against burnout and overextension. If you are already feeling pretty good about yourself and your circumstances, action planning can help motivate your personal greatness.

Reprinted with permission of National Arts Strategies and Jason Tseng.

### *Just play to your strengths?*

The "new millennium" has brought a groundswell of enthusiasm about strengths-based affirmation for children, executives, emerging leaders, graduate students, struggling workers, married couples, and just about any other relationships you can imagine. Admittedly, my research on the best self, authenticity and positive identity development aligns with this strengths-based paradigm. But here's where I depart from the slew of consultants, media personalities and eager celebrants… Take caution toward any book, article, or speech that encourages you to [just] "play to your strengths." (Even though I, too, co-authored a widely disseminated article that bears this catchy title in the *Harvard Business Review* in 2005!!)

What's so wrong with playing to your strengths? Let me clarify. Your focus on strengths is well-placed. Your potential for contributing based on your strengths is infinite. But if your strategy is to just play to your strengths, you will slip into a zone of complacency that is anything but extraordinary. The fact is, most of our strengths are underdeveloped and inappropriately applied. So, contributing from a position of strength means getting out of your comfort zone, by resisting the temptation to rest on your laurels or – at the other extreme – obsess over your weaknesses.

In short, being at your best takes WORK – concentrated, dedicated effort. Your focus should be on GROWING in your areas of strength, and applying them with precision. Think about your favorite athlete. Can you imagine what would happen to their game if they "just" played to their strengths? Serena Williams is being hailed by many as one of the *Greatest Athletes of All Time.*

Serena's record-setting serve would lose speed and power if she didn't keep working on it, training session after training session! She doesn't just rely on serving aces, or assume that she can just show up and execute, and she has been dedicated and exemplary in her craft on the tennis court for over 20 years. We should all model this level of strategic investment in our own strengths, whether they are physical, intellectual, artistic, emotional or all of the above! How easily we can take our strengths for granted… just assuming that we can show up, plug and play! It is painful to watch someone who is truly gifted in an area, but offering less than their best.

If you hear someone declare proudly, *"I am the same person that I have always been!"* this statement should raise a red flag about resistance to growth, change and self-improvement. The process of reclaiming your best self involves continual learning and ongoing self-discovery. You actually don't even know how many strengths you have, or where they can take you, until you begin to concentrate your developmental efforts on getting into your zone of best-self engagement. This means embracing lifelong learning and growth: discovering your best self, being at your best more often, making your best self even better, and bringing out the best in others.

**Focusing on your best self doesn't mean resting on your laurels or becoming complacent in your strengths. Your best self should evolve as you grow more capable, stronger and wiser.**

## *Ignore your weaknesses?*

Reclaiming your best self involves activating your strengths more effectively, so that you expand and enrich your best-self zone of activity. But focusing on your best self and gaining a better understanding of your strengths does not lessen your responsibility to know yourself and manage around your weaknesses. You will face many situations, especially at work, that require you to perform at a reasonable level of competence in areas that are not your strongest. If you fail to demonstrate the requisite competencies of your job, you (and your coworkers) will suffer adverse consequences. If you consistently underperform, you may likely lose your job altogether. Insecurities can lead us to use our strengths as a cover-up for our weaknesses, and to pretend that our giftedness in one area will cancel out our deficiencies in another area. You may be an eloquent public speaker, but if you are not able to collaborate effectively in groups, you will find your career options limited and your social invitations lacking.

Your strengths can generate extraordinary outcomes, but they probably will not out-shine your fatal flaws in core competencies. You need to identify any Achilles' heels—those behaviors, personality traits, and performance deficits that might interfere with your ability to leverage your strengths in a way that creates a positive experience for you and a constructive experience for others. Managing around your weaknesses may involve learning to delegate certain tasks, or putting enough effort into developing new skills in order to achieve an acceptable level of performance. These deficit-based developmental activities are critical. They receive a great deal of attention in training courses, text books, and performance management programs.

But remember, you need to do more than manage around your weaknesses to become your best self. The process of reclaiming your best self doesn't undermine, ignore or cancel out weaknesses, but it shifts the focus onto an equally important area of development – strengths and contributions. Activating your strengths more effectively is a separate and equally important developmental task.

You may find that you have been over-relying on your strengths. There is a fine line between an initial source of strength and the fatal flaw of taking that strength to the extreme. For example, Richard learned that there is a fine line between "attention to detail" and "micromanagement." In Richard's case, he learned that overdoing his attention to detail led to unhappy subordinates who felt micromanaged.

Reprinted with permission of National Arts Strategies and Jason Tseng.

Or, you may be underutilizing your strengths altogether. Consider Simone, who failed to recognize her writing skill as her strength and avoided taking the lead on written communications. She wrongly assumed that everyone had the same abilities that she had, and missed opportunities to help her coworkers strengthen their written presentations and memos. As a result, neither Simone nor her team reached their full potential.

Other fatal flaws include: using intelligence in a way that intimidates others or dismisses their ideas prematurely, relying on your track record in a functional or technical area but struggling to think beyond this narrow area in strategic planning, or using your charisma to manipulate other people. Becoming extraordinary requires a "both/and" formula to round out your developmental agenda: develop core competencies where needed, but strategically invest in learning how to use your strengths most effectively. In sum, you must learn how to balance between your strengths and weaknesses for maximal impact.

## Developing your Strengths

Which do you think would help you to be more successful in life: knowing what your weaknesses are and attempting to improve them, or knowing what your strengths are and attempting to build on them? The Gallup Institute found that the majority of countries favor the weakness approach: only 41% of respondents from the US favored building on strengths, and the percentages were even lower for respondents from Great Britain (38%), Canada (38%), France (29%), Japan (24%) and China (24%). Consistent with these assumptions, we participate in far more developmental activities that focus on weaknesses. This can result in numerous missed opportunities for increasing vitality and value creation.

Let's take this example. A child comes home with the following report card: 2 A's, 1 A-, 1 A+, and 1 C. What conversation does the parent have with the child? The overwhelming (nearly unanimous) majority of participants in my sessions respond, "What happened with the C?!"

Reprinted with permission of National Arts Strategies and Jason Tseng.

Best practices in performance management indicate that we need to focus on strengths *and* weaknesses. It is important for the parent, child and teacher to understand the C and to develop an action plan for improving the C, if the performance in that area is truly below expectations or beneath the student's potential. (Most elementary and secondary courses are designed for students to perform above C-level with effective preparation and study techniques).

In the same way, when we face shortcomings and deficits in our own performance, we should try to analyze them, understand them and make an action plan to address them.

What's missing, though, is our ability to systematically analyze, address and come up with an action plan for building on and leveraging that A+. We lack proficiency in giving and receiving strengths-based feedback. In response to the C, parents, students and teachers alike launch into a host of questions about the personal and social factors that can explain this student's performance: *Did you study? Did you turn in your homework? Are you distracted during class? Did you understand the lectures?* Then, when the time comes to discuss the A+, we offer praise and encouragement. *Great job! Keep up the Good work!* Yet, we don't ask many (if any) questions about the A+. *What do you like about the subject? How did you earn such a high grade in this course? How can we encourage this type of performance in the future? Is there anything we can apply from this subject to the C subject?* We learn much more from questions than statements. Questions are invitations to a conversation, while definitive statements often close more doors than they open.

Yes, we want to be honest and accurate in our self-assessments. We want to have the full picture about our potential and our shortcomings. Working on our weaknesses is part of a commitment to learn, grown and improve. Since each person can learn to be competent in almost anything, it is important to invest in training for core competencies. Knowing our weaknesses is important, because they might undermine our ability to meet the requirements of our jobs. Being blind to our weaknesses can harm our performance, our careers, and our teammates. Managing weaknesses ensures survival (yours and others') by mitigating risks and eliminating deficiencies.

Yet, it is equally dangerous to take our strengths for granted and ignore growth opportunities in these areas. We don't know as much about our strengths as we think we do, and we certainly don't use them as much as we could to produce the kinds of outcomes that we desire. An inordinate focus on performance deficits, personal deficiencies, and limitations can be demoralizing. It is also inefficient to try to become great at everything, because it detracts from focused effort on refining skills that can yield the greatest results. While we are trying to "fix" everything that is wrong with us, we are neglecting those things that we are uniquely suited to do! Instead of leveraging our strengths to create unique value, we focus our attention on working on – or hiding, suppressing, downplaying – our weaknesses. We miss opportunities to excel in the areas in which we might have the most potential, and inadvertently succumb to living a life in which we settle for being good, or perhaps even good enough… But we fall short of becoming our best selves.

A note of caution here, for those who are grow a bit too comfortable claiming credit for their perceived successes. Even if we walked across a high, dangerous, swaying bridge without falling, we wouldn't have accomplished this feat alone. We would still need to acknowledge the bridge builders who supported our journey, the architects who helped chart the course, and the uncontrollable weather conditions that provided us with a calm breeze, clear skies and sunshine rather than the blistering hurricanes that others may have encountered on their journeys across the very same bridge.

Reprinted with permission of National Arts Strategies and Jason Tseng.

Be wary of acting as if you've achieved desired results because of your personal effort, virtue, or intelligence, and *nothing else*. When we take all the credit for victories, we never really learn about why our actions were effective, given the circumstances that we faced. We fail to learn how we are uniquely gifted, because we fail to acknowledge the giftedness of others. Instead of seeing ourselves as solo champions and saviors, it is critical that we acknowledge the joint contributions that others have made toward our success.

## Changing Course

There is a season for everything – a time and place for every encounter. As the saying goes, even "all *good* things must come to an end." In the same vein, there is also a time to call it quits. Why prolong negative experiences unnecessarily? Remaining trapped in situations and relationships that undermine and violate your best self will only harm you. Being paralyzed by pain will only serve the interests of those who seek to hurt or control you. Even worse, you may be harming those who care most about you.

When you are living out of alignment with your best self, you are like a nuclear reactor that has been destabilized and is leaking slow traces of radioactivity into the soil. Your pent up frustration becomes toxic for you and for those around you, and it isolates you from those who you need most.

So, as my Grandma J. used to say during our epic family card games, "If you've got an ace, play it. But know when to hold 'em, and when to fold 'em." In other words, if your costs are too much to bear, and the trade-offs you are making aren't worth it, make it your business to find a new situation. If it doesn't exist, invent it!

*You are an architect of your alignment, responsible for co-creating the conditions that will bring out the best in you and in others.*

Don't remain stuck in misalignment. Seek wisdom at every turn. Know when it's time to change course, or chart a new course, for your own sake and for the sake of your family, friends and community.

Amazingly, when you commit to living in alignment with your best self, the Universe conspires to co-create opportunities that will affirm, grow and stretch you in your areas of strength. Even though the Alignment Quest™ is a lifelong journey, you'll discover more of your best self along the way, become equipped to activate your best self more often, and develop the fortitude and humility to bring out the best in others.

Reprinted with permission of National Arts Strategies and Jason Tseng.

# WORK IT OUT!
## Strengths-based Developmental Agenda
### Exercise 6.1
#### ©Laura Morgan Roberts

**Instructions: The following guide will help you to apply a strengths-based approach to developing yourself and others.**

**Discovering my Strengths.** *When and how do I contribute maximally from a position of strength?*

- ಖಿ Study my successes.

- ಖಿ Proactively seek feedback.

- ಖಿ Identify my key strengths and how to leverage them.

---

**ACTION ITEMS**
**Learning about my strengths:**

1.

2.

3.

4.

5.

---

## Positioning myself to Maximize the Impact of my Strength-based Contributions.

- ∞ Identify the situations in which I make the most valuable contributions.

- ∞ Search for opportunities to reconfigure or shift my role to strategically align my strengths with the organization's mission.

- ∞ Invest in tasks/roles/value systems/organizational contexts that align with my strengths.

**ACTION ITEMS**
**(Re)positioning myself to align with strengths:**

1.

2.

3.

4.

5.

## Developing my Strengths.

- ℘ Demonstrate humility – openness to learn from experience and from others.

- ℘ Develop existing strengths through fine-tuning.

- ℘ Develop new strengths through stretching and trying out new experiences.

- ℘ Practice self-regulation to manage the shadow side of my strengths.

- ℘ Develop strategies for working with my weaknesses (focus on growing stronger, acknowledging my needs, seeking help, building complementarity between my strengths and others' weaknesses, and vice-versa).

---

**ACTION ITEMS**
**Developing my strengths:**

1.

2.

3.

4.

5.

---

# WORK IT OUT!
## Best Self Activation Plan
### Exercise 6.2
#### ©Laura Morgan Roberts

**Instructions: The following guide will help you identify action items for**

- *Knowing: Discovering your best self*
- *Being: Being at your best more often*
- *Becoming: Making your best self even better*
- *Doing: Bringing out the best in others*

**Strategies:**

What can you do differently in the next 2 years to be at your best more often? What can do you to make your best self even better?
- [ ]
- [ ]


What can you do differently in the next 2 days to be at your best more often? What can do you to make your best self even better?
- [ ]
- [ ]


What can you do differently in the next 2 hours to be at your best more often? What can do you to make your best self even better?
- [ ]
- [ ]


What can you do, starting now, to bring out the best in others more often?
- [ ]
- [ ]


What resources are most needed to implement these action steps for increasing your best-self alignment? *Psychological, Physical, Social, Educational, Others?*

ဆ

# APPENDIX

ဆ

# WORK IT OUT!
## Alignment Quest™ Affirmations
### ©Laura Morgan Roberts

*Bringing your Best Self to Life*

### At My Best

- ∞ *I become more authentic.*
- ∞ *I live on purpose.*
- ∞ *I activate my strengths.*
- ∞ *I embrace positive deviance.*
- ∞ *I remain centered.*
- ∞ *I live into my potential.*
- ∞ *I grow stronger.*
- ∞ *I experience vitality.*
- ∞ *I create value.*
- ∞ *I bring out the best in others.*

**At My Best, I am a contribution.**

### Alignment Quest™ Affirmations
### for Redefining Myself

- *Today I will have a love affair with my best self.*

- *Today I will revel in the unique talents and strengths that I possess.*

- *Today I will celebrate my best self moments.*

- *Today I will study my success.*

- *Today I will cherish the knowledge that I am an agent of value-creation.*

- *Today I will remind myself that I am worthy of dignity and respect.*

- *Today I will give myself permission to grow and change.*

- *Today I will adapt to my circumstances with ease.*

- *Today I will embrace development, so that I can grow from strength to strength.*

- *Today, I will celebrate that I am a work in progress, because there is no shame in growth.*

- *Today, I will grow in strength, wisdom, service, and humility.*

- *Today, I will rejoice that my best is yet to come!*

- *Today, I will receive the lessons that only my failures and disappointments can teach.*

- *Today I will put my ego aside.*

- *Today I will let go of my need to be perfect or to be right for the higher purpose of becoming better.*

- *Today I will stop pretending that I'm blameless, so that I can begin the real work of becoming a better person.*

- *Today I will re-narrate myself. I will write new stories of strength, possibility and my unique place in this world.*

- *Today I will turn down the volume on the voices that broadcast my failures.*

- *Today I will cherish the knowledge that, even in spite of my limitations, my best self is enough.*

- *Today I will enter into my best self zone and begin to change the world, one contribution at a time.*

- *Today I will let go of the victim and reclaim the victor in me. I am not the victim of my circumstances until they consume me. As long as I'm still living, I am still fighting. As long as I am still fighting, I'm still living. I have not been consumed.*

ဢ *Today I will be the author of my identity. Even as others try to define me in limited ways, I will have the first and last word on my unique place in this world.*

## Alignment Quest™ Affirmations for Realigning my Actions

ဢ *Today I will sacrifice my time for virtuous action - caring for someone, acknowledging their accomplishments, going out of my way for the sake of uplifting someone else.*

ဢ *Today I will live on purpose.*

ဢ *Today I will forgive myself for the people I have neglected, the tasks I have not completed, and the dreams I have not fulfilled through my struggles to get ahead.*

ဢ *Today I will channel my energy into the activities that will create the most value.*

ဢ *Today I will use my work to bring peace into someone's soul.*

ဢ *Today I will dare to love my work.*

ဢ *Today I will give myself permission to be mediocre in one thing.*

ဢ *Today I will tap into the sources of my strength.*

ဢ *Today I will use one of my strengths in a new way at work.*

- *Today I will pause when something comes easily to marvel at my strength.*
- *Today I will activate my strengths to uplift someone else.*
- *Today I will take on a challenge that I'm likely to fail so that I can discover my strengths.*
- *Today I will be a positive deviant.*
- *Today I will be accountable for my authenticity.*
- *Today I will live my life from the inside out, not from the outside in.*
- *Today I will make decisions based on the results I wish to create, not the judgments that I fear.*
- *Today I will have the courage to pay attention to others' perceptions without losing myself in their judgments.*
- *Today, I will draw the line on identity negotiations. I will decide what I'm willing to change about myself to fit in, and what I'm willing to sacrifice when I stand out.*
- *Today I will distinguish between my style and my substance, and I will help others to do the same.*

- *Today, I refuse to let my image concerns block my growth and development. I will seek the feedback that I need to become my best self.*

- *Today I will leverage the diversity I bring to my work and my world.*

- *Today I will stand out from the crowd for the sake of standing up for my principles. In order to make a difference, I must have the courage to be different.*

- *Today I will reach out to an old friend for a reality check on who I am becoming. Am I deviating too far from my best self in my race to the top?*

- *Today, I will hold up a prism to my life so that my true colors can shine through.*

- *Today, I give myself permission to grow and change. My true self, my authentic self, is dynamic. I don't want to be the same person that I was before "life" happened. I will abide in peace with whom I am becoming.*

- *Today, I will keep it real. Fake it 'til I make it? The only person I am faking out is me.*

- *Today, I will focus on alignment. My values, principles, strengths, purpose, and affirmations will overflow.*

- *Today I will embrace my authentic self, so that I can walk into my best self.*

- *Today I will decide the role that my image will play in achieving my goals.*

- *Today I will honor my principles by standing firm in what matters most.*

- *Today I will peel away my masks of perfection, invincibility, callousness, and detachment. I will reveal my humanity.*

- *Today I will receive the compliment that someone gives to me.*

- *Today I will accept the gratitude that someone shows, whether they are a stranger or an old friend.*

- *Today I will stay connected to my source of inspiration.*

- *Today I will be present in my encounters with others. I will be fully there, not partially there. I will put down my mobile phone while I'm in the company of another human being. I will close my email during a phone call that is important to someone else, even if it isn't important to me.*

- *Today I will create the conditions for someone else to thrive in my workplace.*
- *Today I will reach out to someone in my balcony, and thank them for always expecting the best from me.*
- *Today I will reflect someone else's best self to them.*
- *Today I will speak life to someone else.*
- *Today I will overwhelm my colleagues with positive expectations, interpretations and affirmations, expecting nothing in return but the joy of giving.*
- *Today I will overwhelm my family with positive expectations, interpretations and affirmations, expecting nothing in return but the joy of giving.*
- *Today I will let go of my desire to put someone else down in order to elevate myself.*
- *Today, instead of trying to be the best, I will focus on being my best.*
- *Today I will forgive someone for being imperfect, and learn how to coexist with their whole self so that together, we can become our best selves.*

- *Today I will honor someone else's contributions, even if they outshine my own.*
- *Today I will help someone else to become his or her best self, even if it means their successes will exceed mine.*
- *Today I will coach someone else to be my replacement, to do my job even better than I can do it. I am secure in knowing that I am growing into my next level of contribution.*
- *Today I will pass the baton in the great relay race toward becoming extraordinary. While others are sprinting, I will savor my season of restoration. My next lap is soon to come.*
- *Today I will honor the sacrifices that my ancestors have made to create a world in which my best self can thrive.*
- *Today I refuse to shortchange my world with half-hearted expressions. Within me lies an abundance of gifts, ready to delight the world.*
- *Today, I will find a reason to smile. Even through my tears.*
- *Today I will apologize. Even if it wasn't my fault, it is my responsibility to care.*

&#8500; *Today I will recognize how my actions are inconveniencing someone else. I will stretch myself to help create the conditions in which we can both thrive.*

&#8500; *Today I will remind myself that the road from destruction to affirmation is paved with silence. I will withhold hurtful comments that will tear down someone else's sense of self-worth. They don't need my additional insecurities, blame or guilt trip.*

&#8500; *Today, I refuse to impose my chaos onto other people. My anxiety does not give me the right to destabilize someone else's world or inflict pain upon their soul.*

&#8500; *Today I will focus on my favorite things.*

&#8500; *Today I will bring my best self to work. I will maximize value-creation, by devoting the best of my energy, talents, and principles to my work tasks and work relationships.*

&#8500; *Today I will speak in the discourse of potential rather than the discourse of deficit. I will give more air-time to possibilities and less air-time to my problems.*

&#8500; *Today I will approach my tradeoffs with excitement. I can't have it all, at the same time, but I will soon enter a new season of abundance.*

&#8523; *Today I will take a detour in life. I will get off the straight-and-narrow path. I will take a different route to work. I will imagine a radical shift in my work responsibilities. I will flirt with the possibility of a career change.*

&#8523; *Today I will work faithfully. I will work diligently despite uncertainty, because I believe my service is not in vain.*

&#8523; *Today I will savor my best moment from yesterday before I begin to anticipate the best moment of tomorrow.*

&#8523; *Today I will encourage myself. In a time of difficulty, I will channel peace and stability through my spiritual consciousness.*

&#8523; *Today I will consume purity. I will surround myself with positive messages of virtuous living.*

&#8523; *Today I will be honest with myself about disappointment. I will recognize that others will be disappointed with my choices. And I will still move forward from there.*

&#8523; *Today I will give it another try. Yes, I have failed before, but this time could be different.*

# WORK IT OUT!
## Alignment Quest™ Resources
### ©Laura Morgan Roberts

*What is the Reflected Best Self Exercise?*

- ஒ Available for purchase at www.reflectedbestselfexercise.com

- ஒ *Harvard Business Review* article that describes the exercise:
    - o **How to Play to Your Strengths** by Laura Morgan Roberts, Gretchen Spreitzer, Jane E. Dutton, Robert E. Quinn, Emily D. Heaphy and Brianna Barker. *Harvard Business Review*, January 2005. https://hbr.org/2005/01/how-to-play-to-your-strengths

- ஒ **Why we're Disengaged at Work.** *The GOOP Podcast, featuring Laura Morgan Roberts.* https://goop.com/the-goop-podcast/why-were-disengaged-at-work/

- ஒ **When Strength becomes Weakness.** *Ted #WorkLife Podcast with Adam Grant* that features the experience of participating in the RBSE with Laura Morgan Roberts and Bijou Abiola. https://podcasts.apple.com/us/podcast/when-strength-becomes-weakness/ID1346314086?I=1000436121595

- ஒ **Do you bring your Best Self to Work?** *Making Positive Psychology Work podcast with Michelle McQuaid, featuring Laura Morgan Roberts.* https://www.michellemcquaid.com/podcast/bring-best-self-work-podcast-dr-laura-morgan-roberts

- ஒ Inspirational poem – *your best self is* "**Enough**," by Laura Morgan Roberts. https://www.youtube.com/watch?v=4mpHvhKY0UM

The Reflected Best Self Exercise™ (RBSE™) is the product of work by scholars at the Center for Positive Organizations at the University of Michigan. It had its genesis in Bob Quinn's belief in the benefit of colleagues sharing their thoughts on each other's strengths. After seeing the power it had in executive education programs, he joined Jane Dutton, Emily Heaphy, Laura Morgan Roberts, and Gretchen Spreitzer to form the Reflected Best Self lab in 2002. The team conducted research on the concept, and began using it in classes, with great success. Since then, use of the RBSE™ has spread throughout the U.S., and it is increasingly being used around the world, including hundreds of universities and corporations.

Key references include:

଼ Roberts, L., Dutton, J., Spreitzer, G., Heaphy, E., & Quinn, R. (2005). **Composing the reflected best self portrait: Building pathways for becoming extraordinary in work organizations.** *Academy of Management Review*, 30(4), 712-736.

଼ Spreitzer, G., Stephens, J.P., & Sweetman, D. (2009). **The Reflected Best Self field experiment with adolescent leaders: exploring the psychological resources associated with feedback source and valence.** *The Journal of Positive Psychology*, 4(5), 331-348

଼ Cable, D., Gino, F., & Staats, B. (2015). **The powerful way onboarding can encourage authenticity.** *Harvard Business Review*, November 26, 2015. https://hbr.org/2015/11/the-powerful-way-onboarding-can-encourage-authenticity

## Action implications: Continuing to Discover and Develop Best Selves

- ℘ *Harvard Business Review* article that describes next steps: **To become your best self, study your successes** by Laura Morgan Roberts, Emily D. Heaphy and Brianna Barker Caza. *Harvard Business Review,* May 14, 2019. https://hbr.org/2019/05/to-become-your-best-self-study-your-successes

- ℘ *Harvard Business Review* article that presents ideas for job crafting: **Managing yourself: Turn the job you have into the job you want** by Amy Wrzesniewski, Justin M. Berg and Jane E. Dutton. *Harvard Business Review,* June 2010. https://hbr.org/2010/06/managing-yourself-turn-the-job-you-have-into-the-job-you-want

- ℘ *Harvard Business Review* article that presents ideas for deepening work engagement: **What to do when your heart isn't in your work anymore** by Andy Molinsky. *Harvard Business Review,* July 10, 2017. HTTPS://HBR.ORG/2017/07/WHAT-TO-DO-WHEN-YOUR-HEART-ISNT-IN-YOUR-WORK-ANYMORE

*Additional Articles on Strengths-based Feedback Processes:*

- ℘ Zenger, J. & Folkman, J. **Why do so many managers avoid giving praise?** *Harvard Business Review,* May 2, 2017. https://hbr.org/2017/05/why-do-so-many-managers-avoid-giving-praise

- ℘ Gino, F. **Research: We drop people who give us critical feedback.** *Harvard Business Review,* September 16, 2016. https://hbr.org/2016/09/research-we-drop-people-who-give-us-critical-feedback

- ℘ Raffoni, M. **Honing strengths or shoring up weaknesses: Which is more effective?** *Harvard Management Update.* Article reprint No. U0206B

&#x204A; Kaplan, S. **Reaching your potential.** *Harvard Business Review.* July-August 2008.

&#x204A; Folkman, J. **3 Hard truths about developing your strengths.** https://www.forbes.com/sites/joefolkman/2016/10/21/3-hard-truths-about-developing-your-strengths/#5d6238b2c262

&#x204A; McQuaid, M. **Can you improve your strengths?** https://www.michellemcquaid.com/strengths-development/

&#x204A; Buckingham, M. & Goodall, A. **The feedback fallacy.** *Harvard Business Review,* March-April 2019. https://hbr.org/2019/03/the-feedback-fallacy

*Diversity and Best-Self Development:*

&#x204A; **How African Americans Advance at Work and what Organizations can do to Help.** *Harvard Business Review IdeaCast,* August 27, 2019. https://hbr.org/ideacast/2019/08/how-african-americans-advance-at-work-and-what-organizations-can-do-to-help

&#x204A; **Beating the Odds** by Roberts, L. M., Mayo, A. J., Ely, R. J., & Thomas, D. A. *Harvard Business Review,* March-April 2018. https://hbr.org/2018/03/beating-the-odds

&#x204A; **Women of Color get Less Support at Work** by Washington, Z. & Roberts, L. M. *Harvard Business Review,* March 4, 2019. https://hbr.org/2019/03/women-of-color-get-less-support-at-work-heres-how-managers-can-change-that

&#x204A; **Polish your Professional Image with Better Self-Awareness, Analyze your Social Power, and Get Feedback from Mentors** by Rebecca Koenig. *U.S. News & World Report,* May 22, 2019. https://money.usnews.com/careers/company-culture/articles/polish-your-professional-image-with-better-self-awareness

## ABOUT THE AUTHOR

Laura Morgan Roberts Ph.D. is an organizational psychologist who seeks to activate best selves, cultivate positive identities and maximize human potential in diverse organizations. As a Professor of leadership and organizational behavior, Laura has over twenty years of experience with MBA, Ph.D., and executive courses at the University of Virginia's Darden School of Business, Harvard Business School, Georgetown University, Antioch University, University of Michigan, University of Pennsylvania, and UCLA. Laura also brings strength-based consulting practices to leaders who seek extraordinary performance and personal fulfillment. She is the author of numerous books, research articles, teaching cases, and practitioner-oriented tools which have been featured in *Harvard Business Review* and several other media outlets. Her books include: *Race, Work and Leadership: New Perspectives on the Black Experience* (with Anthony Mayo & David Thomas); *Positive Organizing in a Global Society: Understanding and Engaging Differences for Capacity-building and Inclusion* (with Lynn Perry Wooten and Martin Davidson); and *Exploring Positive Identities and Organizations: Building a Theoretical and Research Foundation* (with Jane Dutton). Laura also composes lyrical expressions to capture questions, insight, and feelings about diversity, identity and relationships that emerge from her research. Laura earned a BA in Psychology from the University of Virginia and an MA and PhD in Organizational Psychology from the University of Michigan.

66367165R00076

Made in the USA
Middletown, DE
06 September 2019